Ageism

Ageism: Past, Present, and Future presents perspectives for understanding ageism and puts ageism in the context of specific social institutions. McNamara and Williamson uniquely provide a number of complementary ways to understand ageism, including social and psychological theories of ageism, economic development, ageism as frame or lens, and ageism at the intersection of various social categories such as gender and race. They then put ageism in the context of mass media, health care, employment, and public policy. This short text is an ideal addition to courses on sociology of aging, social policy, and social problems.

Tay K. McNamara is Interim Co-Director of the Sloan Center on Aging and Work at Boston College. She is the principal investigator of the 2009–10 Talent Management Study, a survey of age-related attitudes and practices among United States employers. She is also the author or co-author of academic articles on a range of topics related to aging and work, such as employer-provided flexible work practices, training of older workers, and volunteerism among older adults. These articles have been cross-disciplinary, aimed at various audiences in academic disciplines sharing an interest in aging and work, such as gerontology, industrial relations, and human resource management.

John B. Williamson is Professor in the Department of Sociology at Boston College. He did his undergraduate work at MIT and his PhD work at Harvard University. He has co-authored or co-edited 17 books, most of which deal with aging issues including two that are gerontology textbooks. He has also authored or co-authored 165 journal articles and book chapters, many of which deal with aging-related issues such as older workers, retirement, Social Security, population aging, intergenerational equity, and old age security policy in various countries around the world. He has served as the chair of the Social Research, Policy, and Practice Section (which made him also a vice president) of the Gerontological Society of America. He served for many years as associate editor of *The Gerontologist* and is currently on the editorial board of five other journals.

Ageism

Past, Present, and Future

Tay K. McNamara and John B. Williamson

Routledge
Taylor & Francis Group
NEW YORK AND LONDON

First published 2019
by Routledge
52 Vanderbilt Avenue, New York, NY 10017

and by Routledge
2 Park Square, Milton Park, Abingdon, Oxon OX14 4RN

Routledge is an imprint of the Taylor & Francis Group, an informa business

© 2019 Taylor & Francis

The right of Tay K. McNamara and John B. Williamson to be identified as authors of this work has been asserted by them in accordance with sections 77 and 78 of the Copyright, Designs and Patents Act 1988.

All rights reserved. No part of this book may be reprinted or reproduced or utilised in any form or by any electronic, mechanical, or other means, now known or hereafter invented, including photocopying and recording, or in any information storage or retrieval system, without permission in writing from the publishers.

Trademark notice: Product or corporate names may be trademarks or registered trademarks, and are used only for identification and explanation without intent to infringe.

Library of Congress Cataloging-in-Publication Data
A catalog record for this title has been requested

ISBN: 978-1-138-20295-5 (hbk)
ISBN: 978-1-138-20296-2 (pbk)
ISBN: 978-1-315-47261-4 (ebk)

Typeset in Bembo
by Taylor & Francis Books

Contents

List of illustrations	vii
Introduction – Ageism: The Elephant or the Mouse	1

PART I
Ageism in Perspective 13

1. Missing Pieces of the Puzzle: Theories of Ageism and Age Discrimination — 15
2. What Do You Owe Your Parents? The Imperfect Link between Economic Development and Ageism — 30
3. Framing Ageism: The Well-Educated Barista in Historical Perspective — 40
4. Ageism at the Crossroads: Intersectionality and the Life Course — 54

PART II
Ageism in Context 65

5. Mass Media and the Segmentation of Ageism: A Look at Stereotypes on Facebook — 67
6. An Ecology of Ageism: Health Care from the Individual Out — 80
7. Peripheral Ageism in Employment: From Explanation to Action — 95
8. Three Ways to Use an Ideology: A Political Economy of Ageism — 113

Conclusion – The Ghosts of Ageism's Future: Five Take-Away Messages 127

Glossary 131
References 138
Index 155

Illustrations

Figures

1.1	Theories of prejudice and discrimination	16
2.1	Value modernization: simplified model	33
3.1	Lifetime generational accounts using generational accounting methods	47
3.2	Cost of four-year college degree in 2014–15 dollars	51
3.3	Percentage of American population living in a multigenerational household	52
4.1	Perspectives on ageism and diversity	55
4.2	Men and women's usual weekly earnings by age (2014)	57
5.1	A model of stereotype segmentation	68
5.2	Percentage of U.S. adults who say that they use Facebook, by age	75
5.3	Percentage of images of men aged 50+ in six magazines	77
6.1	Ecological model of development	81
6.2	Prevalence of three types of pain, by age	85
6.3	Types of elderspeak	87
7.1	Peripheral ageism in the workplace	96
7.2	Explanations for peripheral ageism in work and employment	97
7.3	Rates of call-backs	107
8.1	Theoretical model of social policy and aging	115
8.2	Bismarkian factors	123

Table

1.1	Stereotype content model	25

Boxes

7.1	Case Studies: The Divide and Conquer Approach	109
7.2	Case Studies: The Building Bridges Approach	110
7.3	Case Studies: Correcting Recruitment	111

Introduction
Ageism: The Elephant or the Mouse

What comes to mind when you think about ageism and age discrimination? Do you think of an older worker fired for being "behind the times" or of an older person mocked for being "slow"? When most people think of ageism, they tend to think of big, obvious examples like these. It is no coincidence that perhaps the most iconic image of ageism today is that of the Inuits abandoning the elderly on an ice floe (Gullette, 2010; Savishinsky, 2000). When a practice is decried as ageist, people sometimes refer to it as putting older adults "on the ice," a dramatic gesture that leaves no room for ambiguity. As Gullette (2010) and others have so eloquently detailed, many examples of ageism are relatively overt and dramatic, in which everyone knows it is occurring, but willfully overlooks it. From this perspective, ageism is the "elephant in the room."

If ageism and age discrimination are really so rampant in our social institutions and culture, though, why are people not more outraged? In this introduction, we argue that the elephant metaphor captures only part of the reality of ageism. It is true that there is obvious ageism and age discrimination, examples of people being put "on the ice." However, a more subtle reason that ageism remains pervasive within our culture and social institutions is that it is more difficult to identify and more ambiguous than other forms of prejudice and discrimination. Ageism can be quiet and elusive, more like a mouse in the room than an elephant.

A Thought Experiment: Finding the "Mouse"

Given its elusiveness, how can we find ageism? Imagine you visit a website that asks you questions about your attitudes toward older and younger people. On a scale from 1 to 10, the website asks you, "How positively do you feel toward older people? How positively do you feel toward younger people?" You say you feel somewhat positively toward both age groups, around a 7 on each scale. After all, you think, you aren't ageist! The website then asks you to complete a set of tasks. It tells you to categorize, as quickly as your reflexes will allow, faces as "old" or "young" and words as "good" or "bad." The website then asks you to categorize the same words and faces into "old or good" and "young or bad" categories, and then into the categories "old or bad" and "young or good." After a little practice, you are able to categorize words and individuals according to this method. When you see the word "laughter" you choose "old or good" or "young or good," depending on what the options are. When you see the word "terrible," you choose "old or bad" or "young or bad," depending on what the options are. Maybe you have to think a little harder and longer when the choice is "old or good" than when it is "young or good." Does the difference in the time it takes for you to click each category mean anything?

Researchers using this test, called the **implicit association test**, argue that the difference in the time it takes you to choose between various categories reveals implicit ageism (see ProjectImplicit for implicit association tests). Introduced in 1998 (Greenwald, McGhee, & Schwartz, 1998), the test measures the automatic association between two concepts in your memory. If a person unconsciously associates "old" with "bad," they will be able to categorize old faces into the "old or bad" group more quickly than they can categorize old faces into the "old or good" group. According to this method, the bigger the difference between the two times, the more implicitly biased you are. The underlying logic of the implicit association test is that ageism can be so subtle that you cannot detect it in yourself.

Is Ageism Different?

From this perspective, any form of prejudice can be a "mouse." Implicit association tests have found implicit biases for most categories, such as race and gender. People can be racist or sexist without knowing it. Are ageism and age discrimination really that different? Below we discuss three types of discrimination that can occur with any type of advantaged/disadvantaged group, each of which can be difficult to identify: reverse discrimination, unintentional discrimination, and institutional discrimination. For each of these, we argue that some factors that make prejudice and discrimination hard to identify are consistent regardless of the target group (e.g., women, older adults), but in each case ageism has specific characteristics that further muddy the waters. In all three cases, we focus on **discrimination** (unfair or unequal treatment based on age) because discrimination makes **ageism** (stereotypes or prejudices based on age) visible.

Reverse Discrimination

Reverse discrimination refers to the practice of discriminating in favor of groups that were previously the target of discrimination or, conversely, of discriminating against the historically dominant group. We refer to **age discrimination** as targeting older people and **reverse age discrimination** as targeting younger people. Below, we describe an example of reverse race discrimination (a 2009 case of employment discrimination) and a potential example of reverse age discrimination (senior citizen discounts).

Avoiding Disparate Impact: An Example of Reverse Race Discrimination

In 2003, a white firefighter named Frank Ricci was preparing for civil service examinations in New Haven, New Jersey. He needed to score highly on these exams to advance to lieutenant in the fire department. He quit his second job to have more time to study; paid to have an acquaintance create an audio recording of his textbooks, since he was dyslexic; and spent 8 to 13 hours of study per day using flashcards, practice tests, study groups, and mock interviews. His determination seemed to pay off when he scored sixth of 77 people who took the test, a score that would normally have earned him a spot in a small pool of applicants eligible for promotion to the lieutenant's position. However, the city decided to invalidate the test results, on the grounds that none of the top scorers were black. The city's argument was that, if they allowed the test results to stand, they might face lawsuits under **disparate impact**, a legal doctrine that states that a policy can be discriminatory if it has an adverse impact against a group (in this case, black firefighters) without a legitimate rationale. Ricci and 17 other firefighters who would have been eligible for promotion based on the test results (including 16 non-Hispanic white firefighters and one Hispanic firefighter) sued the city. The decision to invalidate the test results, they argued, discriminated against the firefighters who otherwise might have received promotions (*Ricci et al.* v. *Destedano et al.*, 2009). The white and Hispanic firefighters, according to the plaintiffs, had been the victims of discrimination based solely on their race.

In 2009, the Supreme Court issued a decision on the case, ruling 5–4 that the city had violated Title VII of the Civil Rights Act. The majority decision stated that

> under Title VII, before an employer can engage in intentional discrimination for the asserted purpose of avoiding or remedying an unintentional disparate impact, the employer must have a strong basis in evidence to believe it will be subject to disparate-impact liability if it fails to take the race-conscious, discriminatory action.
>
> (*Ricci* et al. v. *Destedano* et al., 2009)

The case did not rule out the possibility of using intentional discrimination to avoid disparate impact. However, it made it much more difficult for employers to throw out test results to protect themselves against lawsuits.

Senior Discounts: An Example of Reverse Age Discrimination?

Reverse age discrimination is even murkier. For instance, **senior citizen discounts** are reductions in the prices that businesses charge older adults for goods and services, relative to younger adults. They are a form of price discrimination in which businesses offer goods and services for different prices depending on the characteristics of the consumer. From a business perspective, price discrimination is often an attempt to maximize business profits. Because businesses do not have perfect knowledge of what each individual could or would pay, one strategy is to charge different prices to groups of consumers such as students or senior citizens (Khan & Jain, 2005). For instance, a restaurant might advertise that seniors will receive a 10 percent discount off their bill.

There are business motives for having senior citizen discounts, but there is also evidence that price discrimination is only a successful business strategy if the differences in prices are consistent with social norms. For example, imagine a restaurant that allows people taller than six feet to get free dinner on Fridays. Potential customers shorter than six feet might stop going to the restaurant on Fridays, or even altogether, because they felt the special "height" price was unfair. However, imagine that you are over six feet tall. Do you want to go to a restaurant if you believe that it is not treating shorter people fairly? Research has shown that price discrimination, such as senior citizen discounts, are perceived as "fair" if they are consistent with social norms. For instance, Wu, Liu, Chen, and Wang (2012) conducted a study of college students' perceptions of discounts, both those favorable to themselves (student discounts) and those unfavorable to themselves (senior citizen discounts). They found that both senior citizen discounts and college student discounts were less likely to be perceived as unfair than were other discounts because they were consistent with stereotypes. Older adults are usually stereotyped as "deserving" of special treatment, having worked and not received discounts as younger and midlife adults. Students are stereotyped as having low financial resources, and needing discounts as well.

Fairness over the Life Course

The contrast between the two examples given above highlights a distinctive feature of ageism. People stay in the same race or sex throughout their lives, but almost everyone passes through different ages. Rather than focusing on fairness at any given point in time, we might think of fairness over the life course. A younger person who does not receive a senior discount now will later become eligible (i.e., "everyone gets a chance"), whereas a person who is a victim of systematic racism against their racial group will never move into the advantaged group.

Unintentional Discrimination

We define **unintentional age discrimination** in a way similar to Levy and Banaji's (2002) definition of implicit ageism. It is age discrimination that "exists and operates without conscious awareness, intention, or control." Below, we discuss an example of unintentional gender discrimination (chivalry or "benevolent sexism") and a potential example of unintentional age discrimination (elderspeak).

Chivalry: An Example of Unintentional Gender Discrimination

One reason for the persistence of unintentional discrimination is the ambivalent nature of some stereotypes. For example, there is compelling evidence that gender discrimination persists in almost every major social institution, notably in the workplace and in politics. Women start jobs with lower pay, receive fewer resources, and rise to top leadership positions less often than men do. However, most people do not consider themselves prejudiced against women. In fact, Americans tend to view women *more* positively than they view men (Goh & Hall, 2015). How can positive attitudes toward women coexist with discrimination? Glick and Fiske (1996) argue that sexism has both hostile and benevolent faces. Hostile sexism encompasses negative views of women, such as the idea that women try to control or manipulate men for their own benefit. Benevolent sexism instead includes positive or "chivalrous" beliefs about women, including the ideas that "good" women (i.e., those in traditional roles) deserve protection and special consideration. Benevolent sexism is difficult to detect because it manifests itself primarily as kind or considerate acts. If a man opens the car door for a woman, is he sexist or merely being considerate?

The results of a recent study (Goh & Hall, 2015) underlined the difficulty of detecting sexism based on a person's behavior. In this study, researchers asked pairs of undergraduate students (one male, one female) to work together to answer 20 trivia questions and then to have a three-minute unstructured conversation. Each student also answered a series of survey questions from the ambivalent sexism scale that Glick and Fiske (1996) developed. Their interactions were recorded and later assessed for verbal and non-verbal cues such as smiling, patience, and hostility. Male students who were higher in benevolent sexism—those who thought women should be protected, valued, and "placed on a pedestal"—smiled more and were more patient, approachable, friendly, and warm when they interacted with the female student. They gave off many verbal and non-verbal cues about their underlying beliefs, but those cues could represent kindness or friendliness.

The example of benevolent sexism highlights one of the key reasons that discrimination can be unintentional. People who are "benevolently prejudiced" do not see themselves as discriminating against a target group, both because their discrimination takes the form of consideration and because their view of the target group is positive. However, benevolent sexism can have effects as negative as those of hostile sexism. In one recent study of cardiovascular responses to gender discrimination, women had heightened cardiovascular activity following hostile sexism, and impaired cardiovascular recovery following benevolent sexism (Salomon, Burgess, & Bosson, 2015). That is, both forms of sexism had distinct adverse health effects.

Elderspeak: An Example of Unintentional Age Discrimination?

Elderspeak parallels benevolent sexism in many ways. This pattern of speech modification includes: simplified vocabulary and grammar, repetition or redundancy, overfamiliarity (nicknames or terms of endearment such as "honey" or "dear"), third-person reference (calling the older person "we"), a demeaning tone of voice, or speaking loudly, slowly, or at a high pitch (Kemper & Harden, 1999; Ryan, Kennaly, Pratt, & Shumovich, 2000). Williams, Kemper, and Hemmert (2003) provided the following examples of elderspeak as part of a training exercise for certified training assistants: "Good morning, big guy. Are we ready for our bath?" (p. 244) and "Hi, sweetie. It's time for our exercise today. Let's get ready to walk down the hall" (p. 244). You have almost certainly heard elderspeak in the past, but you may not have recognized it.

The prejudice that underlies elderspeak is that older adults are both incompetent and warm (Fisk, Xu, Cuddy, & Glick, 1999), what psychologists Amy Cuddy and Susan Fiske (2002) described as "doddering but dear." In Fiske et al.'s (1999) research, people considered the elderly less competent than most other groups, such as the middle class, students, men, and professionals. However, people also rated the elderly with more warmth than all but two groups ("women" and "Christians"), indicating that older adults—at least when they are perceived as a monolithic group—are among the most liked social groups in American culture. The prejudiced behaviors that this set of stereotypes elicit focus on pity (Cuddy & Fiske, 2002). In the case of elderspeak, the speaker implicitly treats older adults as children who cannot care for themselves or even understand their surroundings without help. Older adults may feel less respected and less competent as a result of elderspeak (Kemper & Harden, 1999). We discuss elderspeak further in the context of health care in Chapter 6.

The Age-Health Connection

The example of elderspeak points to an important reason why ageism is often less easily detected than other forms of discrimination. While older Americans are much healthier than older adults of past generations, rates of disability increase steadily with age (Centers for Disease Control and Prevention, 2009). This means that older adults, in general, are more likely to be frail and to need assistance or accommodation. This can translate to a perception of incompetence that seems to justify practices such as elderspeak.

Institutional Age Discrimination

Institutional discrimination refers to discrimination that is embedded in social institutions. **Institutional age discrimination** refers to unfair or unequal treatment based on age embedded in institutions. Below, we discuss examples of institutional race discrimination (redlining) and institutional age discrimination (age-restricted communities).

Redlining: An Example of Institutional Race Discrimination

Historically, **redlining**—a term that sociologist John McKnight coined to refer to the practice of avoiding investment in low-income or high-minority neighborhoods—is one of the best known examples of institutional racism (Sagawa & Segal, 2000). The history of redlining provides insight into why institutional ageism can become part of accepted day-to-day practice. During the Great Depression (1929–39), falling home values and increased unemployment led to a wave of home foreclosures that threatened to further undermine the economy and to displace hundreds of thousands of families. Family homes were increasingly at risk, with metropolitan non-farm foreclosure rates nearly quadrupling (from 3.6 foreclosures per 1,000 to 13.3 foreclosures per 1,000) between 1926 and 1933 (Ghent, 2010). Various New Deal agencies were created to help save the housing market, among them the Home Owners' Loan Corporation (HOLC). HOLC refinanced loans for struggling home owners, lending up to 80 percent of the appraised value of the home at 5 percent a year, for a term of 15 years. These conditions were considered extremely favorable to homeowners, and even by a conservative estimate, HOLC saved hundreds of thousands of homes from foreclosure. Another New Deal agency, the Federal Home Loan Bank Board (established by the Federal Home Loan Bank Act of 1932), charged HOLC with the task of providing a more "scientific" method for appraising potentially dangerous bank investments. HOLC responded by creating a series of maps of metropolitan areas that identified areas that were considered risky investment locations based on factors such as the proportion of racial and ethnic minorities and low-income residents. Potential home buyers who might have purchased homes in these areas could not obtain loans, leading to a profound disinvestment in many urban areas (Woods, 2012). Additionally, because these loan applicants were more likely to be minorities and lower-income individuals, the use of HOLC's maps amounted to systematic lending discrimination against these groups of individuals. These maps did not create racial and class discrimination in lending, but they did nationalize and institutionalize discriminatory practices.

Redlining in home mortgage lending was forbidden by the Fair Housing Act (Title VIII of the Civil Rights Act), but the practice of geographic discrimination (based on race) has been remarkably persistent, both inside and outside the housing industry. Consequently, the term has been expanded to refer to all forms of geographic discrimination, by which services or goods are denied to residents based on the demographic composition of the area. For instance, some authors have argued that credit card companies can practice redlining (Cohen-Cole, 2011).

Age-Restricted Communities: An Example of Institutional Age Discrimination?

Over the course of the twentieth century, **age-restricted communities** (communities that restrict ownership or renting based on age) have become more common. As early as the late nineteenth century, Florida had become a destination for the upper-class elite. The original "snowbirds"—those who lived in Florida during the winter—believed that moving to a warmer climate could ease or cure many ailments. By the early twentieth century, the snowbird trend expanded to the lower middle class. The Kiwanis Club of Bradenton, Florida, for instance, created a trailer park in 1936 that forbade its residents from holding paid jobs. While the ostensible reason for this restriction was to attract tourists, the end result was that most families with young children could not live there but most older couples could. Like other trailer parks, the Kiwanis Club had social activities, such as dances, plays, and card parties that were appealing to many retirees. In the mid-1950s, perhaps the first formally age-restricted community (Youngtown, Arizona) was created. Buyers were required to be age 65 or older. The idea of age restrictions combined with social activities became the basis for successful age-restricted communities such as Sun City, Arizona (Trolander, 2011). By 2009, 7 percent of households with at least one member who was 55 or older owned or rented a home in an age-restricted community (Metlife Mature Market Institute & National Association of Home Builders, 2011).

The growth in age-restricted communities and the elimination of race-based redlining occurred at approximately the same time. The Fair Housing Act prohibited discrimination in housing (i.e., renting, selling, insurance, and lending) on the basis of race and color, national origin, gender, religion, family status, and handicap status, but did not prohibit housing discrimination on the basis of age. In 1995, the Housing for Older Persons Act specifically allowed the creation of age-restricted communities. Under this law, at least 80 percent of the occupied homes in a housing development needed to have at least one resident age 55 or older to qualify as age-restricted. However, communities often set stricter bylaws on these minimums, promoting controversy. For instance, in one Florida retirement community, the homeowners' association sued an older couple whose infant granddaughter lived with them (Harwell, 2012). Despite this debate, there has been a steady increase in age-restricted communities since the 1990s. We discuss the potential for ideologies such as ageisms to support public acceptance of age-restricted communities in Chapter 8.

Age as "Lifestyle"

One primary difference between age-restricted communities and communities restricted based on any other demographic characteristic is that there is greater cultural acceptance of an appropriate "retirement lifestyle" for older people. Early age-restricted communities were created with the belief that structured leisure activities (e.g., social nights, card games, dances) could replace paid work for older adults. Despite the fact that research has shown the commonality in lifestyle among older adults to be greatly over-emphasized (Roth et al., 2012), the concept of a retirement lifestyle is so ingrained in the design of age-restricted communities that, as Trolander (2011) argues, they could be considered "lifestyle suburbs," communities based around a common lifestyle.

Why Ageism and Age Discrimination Should Matter to Everyone

Above, we argue that three specific age-related factors (i.e., justice across the life course, the age-health connection, and age as lifestyle) make discrimination even more difficult to identify than other elusive forms of prejudice and discrimination. We provided three examples (senior citizen discounts, elderspeak, and age-restricted communities) that are widely accepted, seldom thought of as discriminatory, and—most of all—difficult to confront. The situation may be further complicated by the overlap between these categories. For instance, institutional reverse discrimination can also be unintentional. An eldercare program at work that is only available to employees with 20 years' tenure would unintentionally discriminate against younger workers.

If ageism is so subtle, why should we care so much about it? What should we do about these practices if we identify them as ageist? It is important to keep in mind that while ageism may be difficult to identify, this does not mean that awareness of ageism cannot be raised. Some forms of prejudice and discrimination, such as racism and sexism, are widely recognized, while others such as discrimination related to family responsibilities are just now becoming recognized. Ageism occupies the middle ground. There is a widespread consensus that it exists, but people's conception of it tends to be limited and they tend to gloss over the wide stretch of potentially ageist practices. Below, we describe some reasons why identifying ageism and deciding what to do about it when identified should matter to individuals, employers, and public policy. Additional examples and data will be presented in future chapters, such as ageism in mass media (Chapter 5), in the medical sector (Chapter 6), at work (Chapter 7), and in public policy (Chapter 8).

Individuals

Age discrimination and ageism have concrete, negative effects on older adults. For instance, according to an AARP study (2014), 64 percent of older workers experience or perceive age discrimination firsthand in the workplace. The older workers in this study also reported that they lack confidence in finding a new job, with 16 percent citing age discrimination as a barrier. Their lack of confidence is echoed in another recent study, which finds that 28 percent of older workers reported having experienced at least one type of workplace discrimination including: being passed over for a raise, promotion, or assignment; receiving unwanted assignments; being denied training and development opportunities; being fired or laid off; and getting unwelcome comments related to their age (Benz, Sedensky, Thompson, & Agiesta, 2013).

Ageism also has indirect effects on mental and physical health. Individuals who perceive that they are or have been the targets of discrimination are likely to report that their mental and physical health is poor (Williams, Herman, Gagewski, & Wilson, 2009). As Luo, Xu, Granberg, and Wentworth (2012) describe, the experience of discrimination is stressful and, over time, discrimination "gets under the skin" through mental and physical strain. Their analysis of over 6,000 older adults indicates that everyday, low-level discrimination (such as being regularly treated with less respect than other people) has a stronger negative effect on health than single, major events (such as being fired or denied a bank loan unfairly).

Employers

Age discrimination in hiring and advancement also has real costs for employers. The most obvious of these costs are those associated with age discrimination suits, including legal costs, settlements, and awards. However, the less direct costs of age discrimination are equally important. Employers recognize many of the advantages of older workers, including work experience, maturity, professionalism, and a strong work ethic (SHRM, 2015), but tend to overrate the disadvantages of older workers. For instance, a common misconception is that older workers are substantially more expensive to employ than younger workers. However, due to shifts in the structure of compensation and benefits (including the shift from tenure-based to performance-based compensation, a shift from defined benefit to defined contribution pension plans, and the slower growth in the costs of health benefits for older workers compared to younger workers), employee costs have become substantially more age-neutral over time (AARP, 2015). The end result is that employers who practice age distribution in hiring, promotion, and advancement risk passing over individuals who are a good investment.

Further, as older workers stay in the workforce longer, workplaces will become increasingly age diverse. Like all forms of diversity, age diversity can benefit teams, but only under certain circumstances. For instance, Kearney and Gebert's (2009) study of 62 research and development teams found that when transformational leadership was high (i.e., when managers and supervisors created a vision and then executed that vision in conjunction with their team), age diversity had no significant effect on team performance. When transformational leadership was low, age diversity was associated with poorer team performance. Deal (2006) similarly observed that unfounded age biases can adversely affect the functioning of work groups unless they are properly managed. Understanding these biases can help employers to leverage the increasingly multigenerational workforce.

Public Policy

Ageism also matters to public policy, both directly and indirectly. Directly, our attitudes toward older adults affect whether we think policies that are not strictly age-neutral should be supported or expanded. For instance, in many states drivers over a certain age have more frequent or additional tests for driver licensing (Grabowski, Campbell, & Morrisey, 2004). The logic behind these requirements makes sense on the surface. Older drivers may be more likely to be in serious car crashes than drivers at midlife due to physiological changes and medical conditions (Adler & Rottunda, 2010). Are these requirements driven by fact, or by preconceptions about age? In some states additional requirements start at age 65 (Insurance Institute for Highway Safety, 2015), despite the fact that the fatal accident rates are lowest for drivers age 55 to 74 and highest for those under 35 and over 74 (U.S. Census Bureau, 2012).

Additionally, there are various indirect effects on public policy. Age discrimination in the workplace may cause older workers to retire earlier than they otherwise would have (Schermuly, Deller, & Busch, 2014). This could have negative budgetary effects on programs such as Social Security and Medicare through decreased payroll taxes. Further, to the extent that discrimination negatively affects health (Luo et al., 2012), it may have additional effects on medical costs.

Ageism in Perspective and in Context: A Roadmap of This Book

In this introduction, we have made the argument that—for a number of reasons including the idea of fairness over the life course rather than at one point in time, the age-health connection, and the idea that older adults share a lifestyle or vision—ageism and age discrimination are often more difficult to detect and understand than other forms of prejudice and discrimination. To understand a "mouse" such as ageism, we might need to take different perspectives on the behaviors and attitudes we see in everyday life. Accordingly, the first part of this book presents four perspectives on ageism. These include social and psychological theories of ageism (Chapter 1), economic development as a driver of ageism (Chapter 2), ageism as a frame or lens for understanding the world (Chapter 3), and ageism at the intersection of various social categories such as gender and race (Chapter 4). We intend the four chapters in Part I to provide you with a variety of perspectives for identifying and understanding ageism.

After arming you with these perspectives, we put ageism in context in Part II of the book. While ageism can occur in almost any context, we focus on four major institutions: mass media (Chapter 5), health care

(Chapter 6), employment (Chapter 7), and public policy (Chapter 8). While we suggest a framework for understanding ageism in each of these contexts, you can also apply any of the perspectives introduced in Part I. The perspective you choose will affect the aspects of ageism that you identify, and may change your conclusion about ageism in a given context altogether.

In the conclusion of the book, we look at ageism both in perspective and in context to make the argument that—no matter how elusive ageism may be—we can make some general conclusions about ageism's past, present, and future. We conclude the book by proposing five take-away messages for understanding the future of ageism.

Conclusion

In this chapter, we have made the argument that, while some examples of ageism really are the elephant in the room, there are more examples in which ageism is a "mouse." While many types of ageism (such as reverse, unintentional, and institutional) mirror other forms of discrimination, there are important factors that make age different. These include the possibilities of the idea of fairness over the life course, rather than at one point in time (as in senior discounts), the age-health connection (as in elderspeak), and the idea that older adults share a lifestyle or vision (as in age-restricted housing). We have argued that, while it is difficult both to identify ageism and to decide what to do once we have identified it, ageism should matter to everyone because of its effects on individuals, employers, and public policy. Finally, we have presented a roadmap for the remainder of this book, which looks at ageism in perspective and in context.

Discussion Questions

1. Take the age-related implicit association test at Project Implicit (https://implicit.harvard.edu/implicit/takeatest.html). Do you think it measures ageism? Do you think that most people really have a strong automatic association of young and good?
2. Should age-restricted communities be legal? Would it be acceptable to have a community restricted to adults under the age of 30?
3. Take the ambivalent sexism inventory (www.understandingprejudice.org/asi/). It includes statements such as "Women are too easily offended." If you were to create an ambivalent ageism scale, what statements would you include?

Part I
Ageism in Perspective

This part provides four perspectives for understanding ageism: theory (Chapter 1), economics (Chapter 2), framing (Chapter 3), and intersectionality (Chapter 4). We organize each chapter around a specific question or problem of ageism, including:

- Should we charge older adults more than younger adults for health insurance?
- Do you owe your parents support in old age, financial or otherwise?
- Are older workers taking too many of the good jobs, at the expense of the young?
- Why do actresses' careers usually decline after age 30?

Rather than competing, the perspectives are complementary, each providing lenses suited to understanding different aspects of ageism and age discrimination.

In Chapter 1 ("Missing Pieces of the Puzzle: Theories of Ageism and Age Discrimination"), we consider the practice of charging older adults more for health insurance than younger adults. While we may attribute this practice partly to the higher health-care expenditures of older adults, this cannot be the whole story. Women also have higher health-care expenditures than men, yet few people propose charging them much higher health insurance premiums. We present five theories of ageism and discrimination (cognitive style, group bias, terror management theory, stereotype content, and statistical age discrimination) and ask the reader to determine which—if any—of these theories really explains the health insurance puzzle.

In Chapter 2 ("What Do You Owe Your Parents? The Imperfect Link between Economic Development and Ageism"), we look at the question of filial responsibility laws, laws that require adult children to provide financial support for their parents. We discuss the origin of these laws in the context of economic development, suggesting that our values—including what we think the elderly deserve and what we think we owe them—have depended in part on the shift from pre-industrial to industrial to post-industrial economies. However, there is a large cultural variation, meaning that the link between economic development and values is imperfect at best.

In Chapter 3 ("Framing Ageism: The Well-Educated Barista in Historical Perspective"), we look at the issue of whether older workers are crowding younger workers out of good jobs. We discuss the historical development of three frames, or ways of organizing experience, relevant to the well-educated barista question: compassionate ageism, which views the elderly as poor, frail, and deserving of aid; generational equity, which depicts the elderly as taking more than their fair share of resources; and generational interdependence, which focuses instead on the interconnections and shared interests of generations. In this chapter, we emphasize that while general stereotype processes (as in Chapter 1) and economic development (as in Chapter 2) influence ageism, the precise content of our views of the elderly also depends on the efforts of individuals and groups to promote competing ways to frame our experience.

In Chapter 4 ("Ageism at the Crossroads: Intersectionality and the Life Course"), we look at the example of actresses, who find that they receive fewer roles, less dialogue, lower billing, and less pay as they reach their early to mid-30s. The same is not true of actors. Centered on this example, we discuss three ways to look at intersectionality, the way that experiences and stereotypes occur at the intersection of multiple social categories such as age, gender, and race. These include: double or multiple disadvantage, stereotype buffering, and stereotype subgrouping. We then discuss how frameworks for understanding advantage or disadvantage over the life course help to explain gaps in this explanation.

At the end of this part, consider which of the four perspectives resonates the most with your experience of ageism. In Part II ("Ageism in Context"), these perspectives will reoccur in ways specifically related to particular contexts, including media, work, health care, and policy.

1 Missing Pieces of the Puzzle
Theories of Ageism and Age Discrimination

Imagine a 21-year-old woman who needs to purchase health insurance. She is healthy, but there is always the potential she could be in a car wreck or have another unexpected medical problem. The insurance company tells her that her monthly premium is $200. Now imagine a 64-year-old woman from a similar background. She is healthy, with no history of health problems associated with increased age. The insurance company tells her that her premium is $600. Is this fair? The 3 to 1 ratio between premiums is the current maximum ratio allowable under the Affordable Care Act, and some people argue that this is still unfair to younger adults and may discourage them from purchasing health insurance (Graetz, Kaplan, Kaplan, Bailey, & Waters, 2014). And while a 5 to 1 ratio, with older adults paying up to five times the health insurance costs of younger adults, is a prominent proposed alternative to the current ratio (Blumberg & Buettgens, 2013), there has been little serious discussion of a potentially age-neutral alternative: equal costs for health insurance at every age.

Is the 3 to 1 ratio ageism, age discrimination, or something else altogether? Given the right theory, or proposed explanation, we should be able to better understand why age differences in health insurance premiums are so widely accepted and what, if anything, we should do about them. But theories are most useful when they fit the evidence of real-world situations like the health insurance puzzle described above, and these types of situations often have complications that challenge any single explanation.

In this chapter, we look at the health insurance puzzle through the lens of five theories of ageism and age discrimination, including (1) cognitive style, (2) group bias, (3) terror management theory, (4) stereotype content, and (5) statistical age discrimination. Figure 1.1 summarizes these theories, divided into those that are primarily concerned with prejudice and those that are primarily concerned with discrimination. Theories of prejudice can also focus on the processes of prejudice (how and why prejudice exists) and the content of prejudice (what we actually think about other social groups). The numbers 1 through 5 indicate the major theories that we discuss, in the order we discuss them below. While these are not the only theories of ageism and age discrimination, they represent many prominent approaches.

16 *Ageism in Perspective*

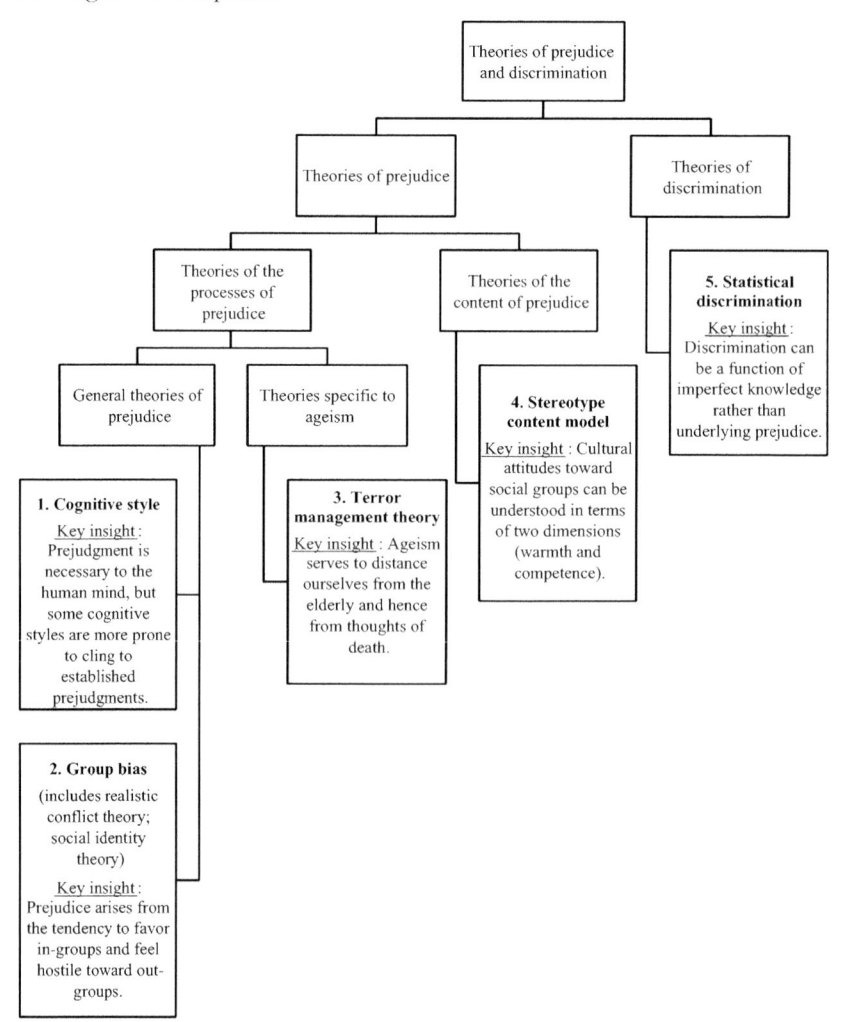

```
                    Theories of prejudice
                      and discrimination
                              │
              ┌───────────────┴───────────────┐
      Theories of prejudice            Theories of
                                       discrimination
              │                                │
      ┌───────┴────────┐                  5. Statistical
  Theories of the   Theories of the        discrimination
  processes of      content of prejudice   Key insight:
  prejudice                                Discrimination can
      │                    │               be a function of
                                           imperfect knowledge
                                           rather than
                                           underlying prejudice.
```

- **Theories of the processes of prejudice**
  - General theories of prejudice
    - **1. Cognitive style**
      Key insight: Prejudgment is necessary to the human mind, but some cognitive styles are more prone to cling to established prejudgments.
    - **2. Group bias**
      (includes realistic conflict theory; social identity theory)
      Key insight: Prejudice arises from the tendency to favor in-groups and feel hostile toward out-groups.
  - Theories specific to ageism
    - **3. Terror management theory**
      Key insight: Ageism serves to distance ourselves from the elderly and hence from thoughts of death.

- **Theories of the content of prejudice**
  - **4. Stereotype content model**
    Key insight: Cultural attitudes toward social groups can be understood in terms of two dimensions (warmth and competence).

Figure 1.1 Theories of prejudice and discrimination

As you read, ask yourself whether any *one* of the theories presented in this chapter really fits what you know about ageism and age discrimination in general and about the health insurance puzzle specifically. The principle of **parsimony** is among the most revered principles in science. Often referred to as Occam's razor (Ariew, 1976), most people understand it as an approach to problem solving that places heavy emphasis on choosing the simplest explanation that fits the evidence. Try to select what you consider the most parsimonious explanation for the health insurance puzzle, based on the theories that we present in this chapter. Does any one theory provide a complete explanation that fits the evidence of the health insurance puzzle? If not, can you explain the missing pieces of the puzzle with another theory? By testing out Occam's razor on a real example, you may come to some unexpected conclusions about which theories of ageism and age discrimination make the most sense to you.

One Among Many? Theories of Prejudice

Theories that explain prejudice in general have an immediate appeal in terms of parsimony. If we can understand age as just one more social category for prejudice and discrimination, like gender and race, then we do not need a separate theory to understand ageism. Below, we discuss two prominent theories about prejudice: theories that explain prejudice in terms of cognitive style and theories that explain prejudice in terms of group bias. These theories, like most other current theories of prejudice and discrimination, have in common that they treat prejudice as a normal state stemming from universal motivations, rather than a pathological state. This point of view has not always prevailed, particularly in certain political climates.

Cognitive Styles: The Shift away from Prejudice as Pathology

Cognitive theories of prejudice and discrimination arose against the backdrop of the psychoanalytic approach of the early 1950s. In the shadow of World War II and the Holocaust, psychologists struggled to understand how fascism had gained so much power on the world stage. They asked why people in Nazi Germany had been so ready to follow orders and close their eyes to atrocities against specific ethnic groups. Their answer was that the "fascist" personality must be pathological. Scholars Adorno, Frenkel-Brunswik, Levinson, and Sanford (1950) referred to this as the "**authoritarian personality**." In a book of the same name, they argued that the personalities of fascists reflected abnormal childhood circumstances. A child subjected to a strict, hierarchical, and authoritarian parent-child relationship, they wrote, tended to form a personality that used subjugation of others and prejudice against vulnerable groups as ego-defense mechanisms. This explanation had the immediate emotional appeal of separating "fascists" from "healthy" human beings. However, it came under heavy criticism in the decades following its publication. Inescapable among those criticisms was that treating prejudice as pathological flew in the face of evidence. Within the "authoritarian personality framework," the widespread and systemic nature of prejudice was inexplicable unless almost all people had defective childhoods. Some degree of prejudice, then, must have been "normal" or at least compatible with a normal human mind.

The Normalization of Prejudice

Psychologist Gordon Allport (1979), in *The Nature of Prejudice*, formulated an influential explanation of prejudice as normal, linking it to cognition rather than psychoanalytic defense mechanisms. He wrote that the human mind needed to think in terms of categories and make prejudgment based on those categories. Separating all kinds of phenomena, including people, into categories was inevitable. Allport famously said, "orderly living depends upon it" (p. 30) because without those categories, it was impossible to learn from the past. Even something as simple as whether to bring an umbrella when leaving the house required prejudgment based on existing categories. We categorized times when dark clouds appeared in the sky as "rainy days" even though there were times when the clouds appeared but rain did not fall. From Allport's point of view, prejudice was a feature of a healthy mind, not just a diseased one.

What was cause for concern, according to Allport, was resistance to contrary evidence. Almost everyone, once they had a prejudgment about a category, would resist a small dose of contrary evidence. For instance, if a person prejudged older adults as "frail" and then encountered an 80-year-old marathon runner, perhaps they would have said "Of course there are some healthy older people, but the rest are frail." Allport likened the appearance of contrary evidence to a breach in the "fence" surrounding that social category, arguing that people had good reasons for hastily "re-fencing" this area. Not only did social norms frequently inform and support prejudgments, it was also less psychological effort to re-fence than to create entirely new, more accurate fences.

Unreasonable Re-fencing as a Cognitive Style

One question that Adorno and his colleagues posed did still need an answer. Why were some people so much more prone to cling to unreasonable prejudice? Allport recognized that not all people were equally hasty re-fencers. Some people would cling more stubbornly to their prejudices, even in the face of repeated contrary evidence and changing social norms. The prejudice-prone cognitive style included a tendency to seek and cling to definite answers and to prefer the familiar and unambiguous. Consequently, this cognitive style built stronger than average cognitive "fences" around social categories (such as "the elderly") and was much less likely to adjust those fences in the face of contrary evidence.

More recent cognitive theories lent support to Allport's contention that, while normal prejudgment was a necessity of life, people with certain cognitive styles were more likely to cling to those prejudgments. For instance, Roets and Van Hiel (2011) argued that Kruglanski's (1989) **need for closure**, a theory originating outside the study of prejudice, mirrored Allport's prejudice-prone cognitive style. Need for closure as a stable individual trait represented a need for "*an* answer on a given topic, any answer… compared to confusion and ambiguity" (Webster & Kruglanski, 1994, p. 1049). This need for closure translated into two tendencies, a tendency toward urgency in finding an answer and a tendency toward permanent adoption of that answer once found. From this perspective, all human minds needed prejudice, but certain minds were more prone to unreasonable prejudice.

A First Look at the Health Insurance Puzzle

Consider the health insurance puzzle from the cognitive perspective. From this point of view, the original difference in premiums results from normal prejudgment. Just as we use an umbrella when it rains, we consider older adults as more likely to need expensive medical care. On the face of it, this makes good sense and seems fair. However, there is an important limitation. The target group is relatively unimportant to this explanation. Allport (1979) says that prejudice is not primarily about a person's attitude toward a group, but rather about the way that person thinks about anything. As we have discussed in the introduction, we often treat age differently. To provide another example, women have higher health-care costs than men, but the practice of charging women more for health insurance was banned under the Affordable Care Act. The same act approved the 3 to 1 ratio for older versus younger adults. The cognitive approach does not offer insight into why we treat some types of social categories such as gender differently from others such as age.

Birds of a Feather: In-Groups and Out-Groups

Unlike the cognitive approach, a second major explanation of prejudice and discrimination does attempt to explain why certain groups are more likely to be targets. This approach posits that we have an ingrained tendency to view our own group more favorably than we view other groups. Byrne (1971) writes in his description of the **similarity-attraction hypothesis** that "birds of a feather flock together," but theories of group bias take this observation several steps further. Birds of a feather not only flock together, they are convinced of the superiority of their own feathers. They sometimes belittle, discriminate against, or even attack birds with different feathers. This image of favoritism toward "our kind" of people and hostility against "other" people seems a particularly condemnatory statement about the human race, but the two experiments we describe below provide less sinister explanations of two sides of the "birds of a feather" hypothesis. First, the "Robber's Cave" experiment looks at **out-group hostility**, unfriendliness or opposition to people in the **out-group**, defined as the group of which the individual does not consider him or herself a member. Second, the Klee versus Kandinsky experiment looks at **in-group favoritism**, preferential perceptions or treatment toward individuals in the **in-group**, defined as the group of which the individual considers him or herself a member.

Robber's Cave: The Origins of Out-Group Hostility

In 1954, two groups of 11 boys spent the summer at a large boy scout camp located near Robber's Cave State Park. They were psychologically well-adjusted 12 year olds, from similar socioeconomic backgrounds and from the same grade in school. Adults separately gave each group a series of goals.

The boys within each group needed to cooperate with their groupmates to achieve the goals. Over the course of less than a week, each group developed a fledgling social hierarchy and sense of group solidarity. They each had a name for their group ("The Rattlers" and "The Eagles"), and when they became aware that there was another similar group at the campground, members of each group became certain that theirs was the "best" group.

Although these two groups of boys may have resembled boy scouts, they were participants in a social scientific experiment about in-groups and out-groups (reported in Sherif, 1958). The experimenters purposely placed the groups into conflict in a number of ways, such as a competition between the two groups in which only one group could win a trophy and prizes for its members. Hostility between the groups escalated with frequent name calling. The experimenters then offered a number of social activities designed to bring the two groups together on friendly terms, such as a celebration with firecrackers on the fourth of July. Rather than defusing tensions, these efforts ended in more name calling and even food fights.

The results of this experiment became the foundation of **realistic conflict theory**, a theory of prejudice and discrimination that viewed hostility between groups as arising from competition for scarce resources. The core argument of realistic conflict theory was that conflict of interest served as the basis for intergroup hostilities. This observation was intuitively powerful because it recognized that there were often tangible reasons for hostilities between groups. For example, if younger adults felt that older adults were blocking their job prospects, hostility toward older adults could take root.

However, close consideration of the experiment left two nagging questions. First, the boys in each group had already created a group identity before the experimenters placed them into antagonistic situations. Scarcity of and competition for resources seemed to explain why hostility against the out-group was strengthened and perpetuated, but not how in-group identity initially formed. Second, the experiment created a clear competition, but in real-world cases prejudice can exist where there is little direct competition. For example, fans of competing sports teams often showed considerable prejudice against each other even though their competition is quite indirect. What explained conflict that appeared to occur for no tangible reason?

Cut from the Same Cloth: In-Group Favoritism

Another experiment looked at this very question. In 1971, experimenters showed 14- and 15-year-old boys slides of paintings by Paul Klee and Wasily Kandinsky. If they preferred Paul Klee's paintings, experimenters informed them that they were a member of the "Klee" group. If they preferred Wasily Kandinsky's paintings, experimenters informed them that they were a member of the "Kandinsky" group. The experimenters asked each boy to distribute points worth money to the other members of the Klee and

Kandinsky groups, with no other information except the group membership. When asked to divide points between anonymous other boys, such as "Member No. 9 of the Klee group" and "Member No. 15 of the Kandinsky group," the responses systematically favored the group to which the boy himself was assigned. There was no interaction between the participants and no known conflict of interest, yet the boys chose to award more money to individuals who liked the same paintings. The authors (Tajfel, Billig, Bundy, & Flament, 1971) argued that this showed a general trend toward in-group favoritism, even in circumstances where there was little basis for in-group identity.

This experiment, along with others that Tajfel and his colleagues carried out, tried to address the puzzle that realistic conflict theory left unsolved. Tajfel and his colleagues argued that realistic conflict theory ignored what was perhaps the single most important "resource" at stake in the Robber's Cave experiment: self-esteem. Each boy in the experiment had a vested interest in believing that his group was superior, because to do so bolstered his own self-esteem. The conflict and scarcity of physical resources exacerbated in-group favoritism, leading to out-group hostility, but even in the absence of any tangible conflict, prejudice flourished. This experiment helped to form the empirical basis of the **social identity theory**, which Tajfel and Turner (1979) formulated specifically as a response to the weaknesses of realistic conflict theory. The central idea of social identity theory was that, due to psychological needs for self-esteem, the existence of two groups, however arbitrary, was sufficient to cause intergroup conflict.

Based on social identity theory, the literature on **relational demography** (Tsui, Egan, & O'Reilly, 1992), which focused on perceived similarity in demographic characteristics, demonstrated how persistent these effects could become when in-groups and out-groups were based on entrenched prejudices, rather than "minimal" characteristics such as what paintings someone preferred or what their original campsite was. Research based on this theory found that, typically, people who were demographically similar in terms of race and gender assumed they had more in common and worked better together. We discuss research based on relational demography in more detail in Chapter 7.

A Second Look at the Health Insurance Puzzle

Consider the health insurance puzzle from the "group bias" perspective as social identity theory and realistic conflict theory define it. From the perspective of social identity theory, the reason we consider older adults an out-group in the case of health insurance is that age, however arbitrary, provides a basis for group bias. From the perspective of realistic conflict theory, the difference in premiums is a reflection of competition for scarce resources. If older adults do not pay more for comparable plans, they might consume a disproportionate amount of the resources available for health care.

There is a flaw in this explanation. Many of the law makers, insurance executives, and other powerful stakeholders involved in the adoption of the Affordable Care Act are at or approaching the 3 to 1 age. If age were truly the basis for comparison, decision makers might have considered older adults the in-group. The 3 to 1 ratio, if it is indeed prejudice, would then be a case of older adults being prejudiced against their own age group. While puzzling in the context of group bias theories, the question of why even older adults are prejudiced against themselves is central to other theories of ageism and age discrimination.

An Inevitable Prejudice: Terror Management Theory

Theories of group bias have proven valuable for explaining why prejudice exists and how it grows over time, but their logic begins to break down when we think about ageism. In terms of group bias theories, ageism is the prejudice on the least solid ground because older adults are frequently prejudiced against themselves. Below, we describe the origins of a different theoretical approach, in which ageism is the *most* inevitable type of prejudice. According to this theory, we cannot help but to fear and dread the old. This dread is one of the guiding principles of our lives and it manifests in our attitudes toward everything from health insurance premiums to prostitution.

Upholding Culture: Does Mortality Matter?

In the late 1980s, 22 judges received a case brief for a woman accused of prostitution, a type of offense typically perceived as morally wrong. After reviewing the case brief, each judge set the bond for the woman's release from jail. However, half of the judges also received a two-item questionnaire in the case brief, to which they responded before recommending the bond amount. They were asked to (1) "Please describe the emotions that the thought of your death arouses in you" and to (2) "Jot down, as specifically as you can, what you think will happen to you as you physically die, and once you are physically dead" (questions cited in Solomon, Greenberg, & Pyszczynski, 2015, pp. 11–12). The difference in bond amount between judges who reflected on their own mortality before making the decision (a mean of $455) and those judges who did not (a mean of $50) was startling. In a parallel experiment, 32 college students recommend a reward amount for a woman who had called a police hotline, at considerable danger to herself, to report that she suspected her neighbor was responsible for a recent series of brutal muggings. Those students who received reminders of their mortality using the survey items described above recommended a mean reward of $3,476, compared to only $1,112 for those who had not received the recent reminder of their mortality (Rosenblatt, Greenberg, Solomon, Pyszczynski, & Lyon, 1989). The core observation—

that when people were more aware of their own mortality, they adhered more strongly to cultural values—became known as the **mortality salience hypothesis**. It received considerable support as one of the most commonly tested hypotheses related to **terror management theory**.

Terror management theory, based on anthropologist Ernest Becker's (1973) book, *The Denial of Death*, argued that human culture functioned to help us manage our fear of death. Of all aspects of culture, religion had the clearest function in the denial of death, because it often promised immortality (Jonas & Fischer, 2006). However, culture related to fear of death in other ways, such as patriotism and adherence to a moral worldview. According to Becker's logic, such adherence helped to bolster self-esteem by allowing people to be part of something bigger than themselves, something that they believed would continue after their deaths. As Becker wrote, "Man cannot endure his own littleness, unless he can translate it into meaningfulness on the largest possible level" (1973, p. 196). When fear of death was more immediate, terror management theory suggested, we adhered more tightly to cultural values as a defense mechanism to protect our sense of self from the idea of death. In the experiments involving the bond for the woman accused of prostitution and the reward money for the police tip, adherence to social norms—both zeal to punish transgressors and eagerness to reward heroes—increased when people were reminded of their own mortality.

Self under Siege: Ageism as a Defense against Mortality

Within terror management theory, older people reminded us of death, so we were prejudiced against them. This was especially true if they embodied what we feared most about mortality. For instance, O'Connor and McFadden (2012) gave each of 240 college students a profile of a man named John Roberts. Born in eastern Wisconsin, John lived an especially unremarkable life. A married man with two children, he worked at Rodin Manufacturing Company and enjoyed walking, traveling, and watching football in his free time. Despite the "everyman" characteristics of John Roberts, not all students received exactly the same profile. In total there were eight possible "John Roberts" profiles: four profiles in which John was 29 years old (one was healthy, one had no health information included, one had arthritis, and one had progressive dementia) and four profiles in which John was 71 years old (again, one was healthy, one had no health information included, one had arthritis, and one had progressive dementia).

The experimenters also asked the students to do a word-completion task, a sort of puzzle where the students had to complete word fragments as real words. One item, for instance, asked students to complete the following word: C O F F _ _. Two common words were possible: "Coffee" (death-neutral) and "Coffin" (death-related). Overall, 6 of the 18 word-completion tasks had both death-neutral and death-related potential completions. The logic of the completion task was that the thoughts that were currently most accessible to the person's mind would influence the words chosen. The more words that the student completed in a death-related way, the more accessible the experimenters believed their thoughts about death were to their minds. The students who had read about the older version of "John" had higher death-thought accessibility than those who read about the younger version of "John." And, of all eight profiles, the older version of "John" who had dementia prompted the most thoughts about death. Mental infirmity among the old appeared to be a trigger for death thoughts.

Other studies provided more direct evidence that the association of the elderly—especially the frail elderly—with death translated into ageism. In one study, experimenters asked some college students to write a narrative about death, while asking other college students to write a narrative about dental pain. Compared to students who wrote about dental pain (a control group), students who wrote about death subsequently reported more negative views of the elderly (Martens, Greenberg, Schimel, & Landau, 2004).

Terror management theory provided one answer to the question of what Nelson (2011) called the "strange case of prejudice against the older you." We were ageist to distance ourselves from what we subconsciously saw as our older selves. By reminding us of our mortality, older adults—particularly those who were ill or frail, challenged our self-esteem. According to this argument, the more that death was "on our mind" the more ageist we behaved (Martens, Goldenberg, & Greenberg, 2005).

A Third Look at the Health Insurance Puzzle

Consider the health insurance puzzle from the perspective of terror management theory. According to this theory, we are willing to charge older adults more for the same health insurance primarily because older adults, especially if they become sick and need that insurance, remind us of our own mortality. Even though women also have higher medical costs, we are less willing to charge them more for health insurance because the type of medical costs that women often incur (e.g., pregnancy) reminds us less of death than the type of medical costs that older adults often incur (e.g., treatment for dementia). This is appealing because it explains the difference between how we treat gender and how we treat age. Terror management theory, however, has at least two major limitations. First, it does not account well for cultures that revere the elderly. Second, it does not account well for our attitudes toward different groups of the elderly, except for the delineation between the frail (who remind us of death more) and the healthy (who remind us of death less). Below, we detail a fourth major strand in the literature on ageism and age discrimination that helps to address these concerns using a cultural approach.

Through the Eyes of Culture: The Content of Ageism

The first three major theories focus on stereotype processes, processes that are generally stable over time and context. However, they say relatively little about stereotype content: what we actually think. There are many unfavorable characteristics that we could assign to out-groups, many ways of distancing ourselves psychologically from the elderly, and many types of cognitive fences we could erect, yet the theories we have discussed thus far pay little attention to the content of prejudices. Cuddy and Fiske (2002) argue that we tend to think of the content of stereotypes as random, varying over time and context so much that it is not worth studying and that this often gives short shrift to some of the most important aspects of stereotyping.

Cultural Differences in Ageism

Fiske et al.'s (1999) **stereotype content model** helped put these stereotypes into perspective. Fiske and her colleagues argued that stereotypes have two dimensions: competence (meaning we thought of the target group as independent and skillful) and warmth (meaning we thought of the target group as trustworthy and likeable). For each possible cluster, an underlying characteristic prejudice formed the basis for the stereotype's content. As shown in Table 1.1, in the case of the elderly, the incompetent-warm stereotype elicited a prejudice of pity; the rest of the stereotype content (such as "The elderly are frail" and "The elderly are lonely") built on this basic prejudice (Cuddy & Fiske, 2002).

The content of these stereotypes has varied widely across cultures and through history, with evidence suggesting that attitudes toward older adults tended to be more positive in traditional cultures than they later became. Western culture since the Industrial Revolution, which increasingly valued individualism and youth, fostered negative views of

Table 1.1 Stereotype content model

	Cold	*Warm*
Incompetent	Incompetent-cold cluster Example: welfare recipients Prejudice: contempt Subtype: senior citizen	Incompetent-warm cluster Example: elderly Prejudice: pity Subtype: grandmotherly elderly
Competent	Competent-cold cluster Example: rich Prejudice: envy Subtype: elder statesman	Competent-warm cluster Example: the middle class Prejudice: admiration Subtype: unknown

Source: based on Cuddy et al. (2005)

the elderly. Consequently, among young adults the stereotype of the elderly as warm and incompetent spanned many modern cultures, including those in which traditional cultures had been extremely collectivistic (Cuddy, Norton, & Fiske, 2005). For instance, Yun and Lachman (2006) found that Koreans, from a culture which traditionally revered the elderly, reported greater fear of the elderly than Americans. There is evidence that the incompetent-warm stereotype has not eclipsed traditional cultural views entirely. Bergman, Bodner, and Cohen-Fridel (2013) found that Arabs, who traditionally saw the elderly as leaders within the expanded family, maintained relatively positive attitudes toward older adults. Even within Western cultures (e.g., United States, Germany, as discussed in McConatha, Schnell, Volkwein, Riley, & Leach, 2003), there was substantial variation between cultures despite an overall trend toward ageism.

Not Our Kind of Old Person: Elderly Subtypes

Think for a moment about the stereotypes you may have heard about the elderly. These might include the grandmother who bakes cookies for her grandchildren, the frail and old-fashioned recluse, and a distinguished and intelligent leader. You probably have clear images of those stereotypes, yet they conflict with each other. For decades, researchers have noted this divergence in elderly stereotypes, positing that there are various subtypes. Brewer, Dull, and Lui (1981) called the subtypes above the "grandmotherly" subtype the "senior citizen" and the "elder statesman," respectively. As shown in Table 1.1, within the stereotype content framework, the grandmotherly type was incompetent and warm, the senior citizen was incompetent and cold, and the elder statesman was competent and cold (Cuddy & Fiske, 2002).

A Fourth Look at the Health Insurance Puzzle

Consider the health insurance puzzle from the perspective of culture. According to this theory, we might attribute the difference in health insurance premiums to our low perception of elderly competence. We like the elderly (high warmth), but we think their health costs are likely to be high due to how frail they are and how little they are able to take care of themselves (low competence). This explanation may be part of the story, but it flies in the face of what we know about subtypes. For instance, we believe some elderly to be both cold and competent and others to be warm and incompetent. Is it possible that we treat all elderly alike, not because we think they are all alike, but because we can't tell the difference? Below, we discuss a theory from labor economics that makes that claim.

Discrimination without Ageism: The Costs of Imperfect Knowledge

Economist Gary Becker, in his 1957 book *The Economics of Discrimination*, took an economic approach to the same discrimination problem that was troubling psychologists, sociologists, and anthropologists. Responding mostly to racial discrimination in the labor market, he argued that discrimination has costs, and not only to the targets of discrimination. Firms who discriminated against the best candidates paid more to reach the same productivity, because they needed to hire more people or pay people more for the same job. Becker concluded that certain people had a taste against associating with certain target groups, and they behaved as if associating with that group carried an invisible, non-pecuniary cost that outweighed the pecuniary benefits of hiring the "best person for the job." This type of discrimination, known as **taste-based discrimination**, was something of a black box within which all processes of and content of prejudices existed. Becker's theory remained powerful because it opened the door to modeling the real costs of discrimination, but by the 1970s other economists began to look at the question of discrimination by rational and unprejudiced actors. Could discrimination ever pay?

The Power of Imperfect Knowledge

In the early 1970s, Phelps (1972) and Arrow (1973) published complementary articles that became the basis for the concept of **statistical discrimination** (Fang & Moro, 2010). Statistical discrimination referred to cases in which actors were rational and unprejudiced but nonetheless discriminated. They substituted group averages for individual information, which was often difficult or impossible to obtain. The core of the statistical discrimination argument was the idea that knowledge was often imperfect. Phelps (1972) argued that, if individual information was not practically available, a rational actor would instead substitute group averages. For individuals who performed better than those group averages, this would amount to discrimination, but a discrimination with no underlying taste-based prejudice. For instance, imagine an employer needed to choose between hiring a 70-year-old job applicant or a 40-year-old job applicant. Both applicants said that they planned to stay for the duration of the project for which they were hired, but the employer felt unsure of these statements. The employer believed that 70 year olds had lower labor force attachment than 40 years olds, so that the average 70 year old would be more likely to leave the position early than the average 40 year old. Hence, the employer substituted knowledge about group averages for what they did not know: the applicants' actual intent to stay on the job. According to Phelps, this was discrimination, but a discrimination that did not involve what we usually thought of as prejudice.

Arrow (1973) further showed how employer perceptions of different groups became self-fulfilling policies which caused a lack of individual investment in certain skill sets. For instance, imagine that the position for which the employer was considering the 70-year-old and 40-year-old applicants involved expertise in social media. The employer might have assumed that on average 70-year-olds had less expertise in technology, and offered the job to the 40-year-old. But over time, the expectations of employers that older adults were unsuited for certain types of jobs might cause older workers to stop developing those skills. They did not have the same access to the jobs that would require those skills, due to statistical discrimination. Even when they did have those skills, employers discriminated against them as if they did not have them. There was little incentive to them to develop and maintain those skills.

A Fifth Look at the Health Insurance Puzzle

Consider the health insurance puzzle from the perspective of statistical discrimination. Decision makers believe older adults incur higher medical costs than younger adults. They then decide on the 3 to 1 ratio, even though some older adults will have higher medical costs and others will have lower medical costs than the average. As with each theory that we present in this chapter, statistical discrimination has some limitations. For instance, it still does not explain why we find the 3 to 1 ratio by age acceptable, but not a ratio by gender. However, it does offer a compelling explanation about how discrimination can stem from "hard facts" (or what we think are hard facts) rather than simply liking or disliking a social group.

Conclusion

In this chapter, we have looked at a specific topic—the health insurance puzzle—through the lenses of five different theories of ageism and age discrimination: cognitive style, group bias, terror management, stereotype content, and statistical discrimination. The principle of parsimony would urge us to find the simplest explanation that fits the evidence, but what you probably found is that each of the theories both provided compelling insights and left frustrating gaps. The unfortunate truth is that simple isn't always right, because sometimes no simple explanation fits the evidence. As the mathematician Karl Menger (1979) said in his aptly named *Law against Miserliness*: "It is vain to try to do with less what requires more" (p. 106) If a theory does not fit the evidence of ageism and age discrimination, then however elegant and convincing the theory seems on the surface, something more is needed. As you read the remainder of the book, consider the theories discussed in this chapter and decide which theories—if any—fit the evidence of what you will learn about real examples of ageism and age discrimination. You may come to the conclusion that one or two of the theories presented in this chapter fit the evidence better than others. Or, you may come to the conclusion that, while some or all of these theories bring valuable insights, there are still missing pieces of the puzzle.

Discussion Questions

1. If statistical age discrimination is based on "hard facts," do you think that it is more acceptable ethically than discrimination based on irrational prejudices?
2. The way in which the experimenters successfully reduced prejudice in the Robber's Cave experiment was a series of tasks that required both groups to work together. Do you think that a similar project, in which older and younger adults were required to work together to achieve a goal, would reduce ageism? Why or why not?
3. Take close look at Table 1.1. You'll notice that none of the elderly subtypes fit the warm and competent cluster. Is there an elderly stereotype considered both likeable and independent? If not, what explains this missing stereotype?

2 What Do You Owe Your Parents?
The Imperfect Link between Economic Development and Ageism

In 2007, Pennsylvania restaurant owner John Pittas received a very unexpected bill. A nursing rehabilitation center billed him over 90,000 dollars for expenses his mother had incurred while recovering from a car accident. Pittas' mother moved to Greece before receiving official Medicaid approval to cover her stay in the center. The center then sued her son under **filial responsibility law**, which typically placed financial responsibility for supporting impoverished older adults on their children. A Pennsylvania court ruled that Pittas was in fact responsible for paying the bill, despite the unusual circumstances (Superior Court of Pennsylvania, 2012). Only a handful of recent cases had successfully used these laws, and of those Pittas' case was unique in that the court did not say he had done anything wrong. He had not attempted to hide his mother's assets or to request extra care through the center. Yet, the court still ruled in favor of the center simply because his mother could not pay, and he could.

Filial responsibility laws, originating in a time before the entitlement programs that now offer modest income and medical insurance to older adults, provide a window into past incarnations of ageism. They draw on social norms indicating that the elderly deserve financial support from their relatives, and that their relatives owe them this support. But social norms about whether the elderly deserve obedience, deference, financial support, pity, or no special treatment at all reflect our stereotypes about age and aging, and these stereotypes can and do change over time. One of the major factors behind these changes is a country's level of **economic development**, a broad term for the stage, state, or level of an economy as it relates to the well-being of the people living within it.

In this chapter, we take a different approach than in Chapter 1, which focused primarily on stereotype processes. We look at stereotype content, arguing that the **value modernization framework** (Inglehart & Welzel, 2005) provides a particularly useful way to understand the imperfect link between economic development and ageism. Below, we outline the logic of value modernization, provide historical examples of its major trends, and then return to the question of what we owe the elderly in light of these trends.

Value Modernization: The World Values Study

At the core of the value modernization framework is the idea that, while economic development is one of the major drivers of values, unique cultural characteristics can also shape our values in dramatic ways. Below, we: (1) discuss how the value modernization framework responds to earlier theories that link values primarily to level of economic development; (2) outline the general argument of the value modernization framework; and (3) reflect on the importance of cultural differences in attitudes toward the elderly, using examples from pre-literate societies.

From Modernization to Value Modernization

The value modernization framework grew out of earlier social theories that saw economic development as the primary driver of values. Notably, **modernization theory** proposed that the economic changes accompanying industrialization triggered the development of modern social structures and norms, and **convergence theory** proposed, in line with sociologist Talcott Parsons' (1960) structural functionalism and economist Clark Kerr and colleagues' (1960) logic of industrialism argument, that economic conditions caused societies to become more structurally and culturally similar over time. One key argument of modernization theory was that **industrialization**, the transition from agricultural and commercial economies to industrial economies, necessitated the development of the **welfare state**, the system through which the government attempted to promote the social and economic well-being of vulnerable individuals. The weakening of family ties, combined with the hazards involved in the industrial workplace, meant that most people who became unable to work due to old age or disability could no longer rely on their families or on charity alone, making the development of government policies critical for vulnerable populations (Kerr, Dunlop, Harbison, & Myers, 1960). From this perspective, programs such as Social Security and unemployment were hallmarks of successful development.

Sociologists Donald Cowgill and Lowell Holmes (1972; Cowgill, 1974) extended the insights of modernization theory to attitudes toward and treatment of the elderly. They argued that industrialization eroded the traditional bases of support for the elderly in numerous ways. Mass education reduced the perceived value of accumulated wisdom and knowledge as sources of authority for older adults, while concentrating the skills that employers valued in the younger population. Advances in public health and medical practice meant that people lived longer but, because employers typically preferred to hire younger workers, were less likely to remain employed as they aged. The development of factories drew younger workers to urban areas, increasing the geographic distance between the elderly and their kin and undermining systems of intergenerational support.

Because of these trends, Cowgill and Holmes (1972) wrote, industrialization led to a sharp decline in the status of and attitudes toward the elderly. Earlier positive ageisms in which the elderly were respected for their wisdom gave way to negative ageisms in which people viewed them as deserving of charity, but frail, needy, and pitiable.

Ageism through a Value Modernization Lens

The key insight of modernization theory—the link between level of economic development and cultural values—is difficult to dispute (Myles & Quadagno, 2002), but the details of the theory have been under attack almost since its inception. The more formal, stricter, and "stronger" variants of modernization theory, such as Cowgill and Holmes' (1972) clear identification of salient factors underlying industrialization, are also the most vulnerable to contrary evidence and criticism. By arguing that societies converge in culture and by treating economic development as the single most important driving factor in values, modernization theory can ignore vast cultural differences.

The value modernization framework attempts to adapt modernization theory to these criticisms by emphasizing the imperfection of the link between economic development and values. Rather than focusing on overall convergence to a single modern society, economic development shapes only the most general trends. Figure 2.1 shows a simplified model of the two trends that the value modernization framework proposes, adapted to our analysis of ageism.

The Authority Shift

The value modernization framework suggests that cultures fall on a continuum from traditional to secular-rational values. As shown in Figure 2.1, traditional values prevail at the lowest levels of economic development. Individuals in these cultures are likely to believe that religion is "very important in... life" and that one of their "main goals in life has been to make his/her parents proud" (Inglehart & Baker, 2000, p. 26). The elderly typically benefit from traditional values because people respect them for their wisdom and knowledge. But as people gain control over the forces of nature and have scientific explanations for physical phenomena, they are less likely to emphasize traditional sources of authority (Inglehart & Baker, 2000). For the elderly, the shift toward secular-rational explanations weakens their authority. Historically, the largest **authority shift** occurred during the shift from agricultural and commercial to industrial economies.

The Well-Being Shift

The value modernization framework includes a second major shift, from survival values to self-expression values. As shown in Figure 2.1, at lower levels of economic development, individuals tend to focus on survival

What Do You Owe Your Parents? 33

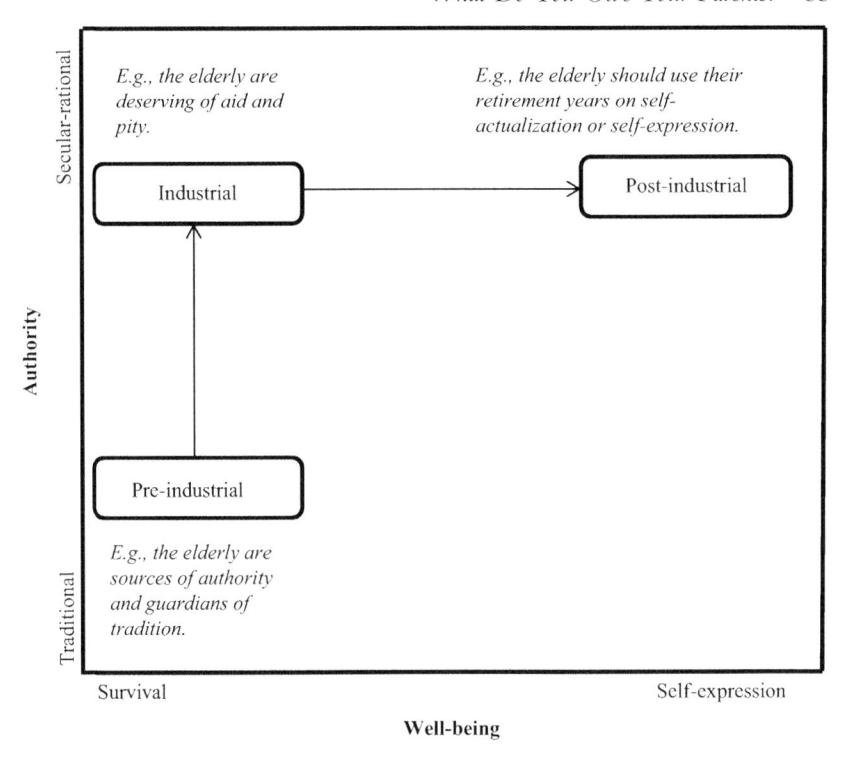

Figure 2.1 Value modernization: simplified model

values, due to the difficulty of ensuring physical and economic security. But at higher levels of development, the advent of service economies increases the cultural importance of self-expression. People living in countries at higher levels of development are more likely to value imagination in children, less likely to agree that they "must always love and respect one's parents regardless of their behavior" (Inglehart & Baker, 2000, p. 27), and more likely to promote tolerance for the views, lifestyles, and self-expression choices of others (Inglehart & Baker, 2000). Historically, the largest **well-being shift** occurred during the shift from industrial to post-industrial economies.

Cultural Variation: The Example of Pre-Literate Societies

While economic development shapes general trends in values, in some cases culture may be just as or more important. Consider, for example, the following three tribal cultures at the lowest levels of economic development: the Ojibwe, the Chukchi, and the Khoi. Among the Ojibwe of North America (a part of the larger Anishinaabe group), the term for an older person was *gichi anishinaabe*, meaning "great person" (Treuer, 2010). Andrew Makade-bineshi Blackbird's written "commandments" of Anishinaabe life instructed the young to "Hold thy peace, and answer not back, when thy father or thy mother or any aged person should chastise thee for thy wrong" (cited in McNally, 2009, p. 5).

Within Ojibwe culture, the elderly deserved deference and obedience for their wisdom. Among the Chukchi, an indigenous people that subsisted by hunting reindeer or sea mammals in Siberia, elderly people who considered themselves a burden would opt for voluntary death. Members of their village sang, drank, and feasted in honor of an elderly person who had decided to die (de Beauvoir, 1996 [1970]), a tradition that persisted in limited form into the twentieth century (Willerslev, 2009). Deference to the elderly drew on their willingness to volunteer for death in the face of the pressures of physical survival.

Among the Khoi of Southern Africa, the elderly did agricultural work until their physical health no longer allowed it. Then, they shepherded younger members of the community through rites of passage such as marriage and widowhood. The Khoi traditionally considered people who were between stages of life to be dangerous to themselves and others, but believed that people who had passed through those specific transitions were immune from this danger (de Beauvoir, 1996 [1970]). Once an elderly person could not perform any function in society, the Khoi might abandon them in huts with a small amount of food and water while the rest of the tribe moved on.

While we cannot draw firm conclusions about the pre-literate societies of the distant past based on what we know about customs of present-day or recent cultures, a logical fallacy that Arland Thornton (2005) terms **reading history sideways**, the extremely varied examples of the Ojibwe, Chukchi, and Khoi allow us to gain insight into general trends in ageism. As the value modernization framework would suggest, at the lowest levels of economic development, traditional and survival values prevail. These observations are consistent with other observers, such as Jared Diamond (2012), who notes that wisdom or knowledge is among the most powerful and widespread resources of the elderly in pre-literate societies, and Simone de Beauvoir (1996 [1970]), who, when contemplating the extreme neglect of the elderly among some impoverished tribes, concludes that "When poverty reaches the extreme point, it is the deciding factor" (p. 47). Despite these common threads, the way that cultures fuse survival and traditional values is extremely diverse. The Ojibwe and Khoi allocate high importance to the elderly as unique sources of wisdom, but most people would agree that the outlook for the elderly in the Ojibwe example is more positive. The Chukchi and Khoi cultures reflect the extreme difficulty of physical survival, but have unique ways of reconciling respect for the elderly as keepers of tradition with the killing of elderly who become burdens. Pre-literate societies, due to particularly low levels of economic development, represent the clearest examples of traditional and survival values.

Value Modernization: A Historical Perspective

The value modernization framework seems to provide a parsimonious explanation of ageism in pre-literate societies. Ageism in these societies is a set of unique cultural values that reconciles a preoccupation with the harsh difficulties of physical survival and recognition of the potential power of the elderly as sources of knowledge. But when we look at societies at even slightly higher levels of economic development, the story is less clear. We argue below that we can observe two trends (the authority shift and the well-being shift) over the past 500–600 years, but the trends tend to develop less evenly than Figure 2.1 would predict.

The Authority Shift

Historically, in the United States and Europe, the shift from traditional to secular-rational authority occurred gradually, with challenges to the power of older adults as sources of unique and valued knowledge arising centuries before the Industrial Revolution. For instance, prior to the 1500s, Italians learned trades through apprenticeship or at reckoning schools. Apprenticeship allowed older and more established tradesmen to pass down their knowledge, while reckoning schools sprang from the need of a growing merchant class to keep accurate ledgers and accounts (Swetz, 1987). Both methods required younger adults to learn directly from older adults. But beginning with the publication of textbooks on printing presses, such as the 1478 *Art of Calculation*, younger adults could learn arithmetic, including algorithms such as how to add and subtract amounts of money, without an older teacher. The error-free and widespread distribution of technical textbooks marked a fundamental change in the way the younger generation gained skills and information (Eistenstein, 1983), undermining a major source of the traditional authority of older adults.

In spite of this gradual erosion, reverse ageism (in which the elderly were viewed as wiser, more reliable, and more ethical than the young), persisted in some form for centuries. For instance, in colonial America, "boards of elders" governed churches, a practice that expanded on the respect for elders manifest in the Bible. A reliance on agriculture meant that the elderly owned or had power over a key economic resource. The importance of experience in the skilled trades, such as masonry or blacksmithing, gave older workers further power (Palmore, 1999). While the positive ageism toward the elderly stemmed from their accumulated knowledge, wisdom, and experience, it was maintained by and crystallized in social institutions until the advent of industrialization.

Industrialization accelerated the shift to secular-rational forms of authority through mechanisms such as mass education. Prior to the introduction of mass education, many children did not attend school regularly due to the demands of agricultural life. Those who did attend learned basic literacy and calculation. Pioneered in the early 1830s by Prussia, compulsory mass education shifted the focus from basic literacy to the host of scientific and technical skills that employers needed for growing industries (Seavoy, 2006). These knowledge and skills became concentrated among the young, while the knowledge of older adults, based on a lifetime of experience, became less valued. Employers consequently favored younger adults for more prestigious, stable, and well-paid jobs, leaving older adults concentrated in lower-status occupations or unable to find employment. Whereas other forms of modernization theory linked the development of negative ageism to a variety of specific factors, the value modernization framework drew our attention to the waning of traditional values and the rise of secular-rational values as the key factor.

The Well-Being Shift

The value modernization framework suggests that the shift from industrial to post-industrial economies carries with it a redefinition of well-being. Rather than focusing on physical well-being, people become interested in self-expression or self-actualization. If true, we are still in the process of this cultural shift. There is some evidence that self-actualization or self-expression could become a key component of a new stereotype of the elderly.

Consider, for instance, the Red Hat Society, aimed specifically at older women. In the late 1990s, an American artist named Sue Ellen Cooper celebrated her friend's 55th birthday with an unusual gift. Referring to the Jenny Joseph poem that warned the reader "When I am an old woman I shall wear purple/With a red hat which doesn't go, and doesn't suit me" (Joseph, 2001 [1962]), Cooper gave her friend a red hat to celebrate what she saw as the positive side of old age: a freedom from expectations to be practical, reliable, and responsible. In the coming years, she gave red hats to more of her friends as they reached the age of 50, a practice that became the core of the "Red Hat Society." With tens of thousands of chapters, the Red Hat Society became a large for-profit business, but the core message of the society still hinged on freedom from responsibilities and the chance to "be yourself." Members of the society, most of whom were older women, put on annual parties, at which they played with hula hoops, kazoos, and paddle balls; participated in Easter egg hunts; and dressed up in extravagant clothing (Barrett & Naiman-Sessions, 2016). Self-expression meant abandoning the seriousness and restraint that characterized much of their adulthood.

The Red Hat Society focused primarily on women in Anglo cultures, but self-expression meant vastly different things for elderly in other cultures. For instance, traditional Indian multigenerational households had a two-phase system of intergenerational reciprocity, in which parents supported children in the initial phase, then adult children "repaid" their debts to their parents through sevā (Lamb, 2000), the respect and service due to the aged. Because most acts of sevā could only be performed in person, the rise of old-age homes became an emblem of the disintegration of traditional culture. A small but growing number of old-age homes responded to this with an age-old idea in new clothing: the old-age home as an ashram, or spiritual retreat, through which older adults could achieve self-actualization (Lamb, 2009). Traditionally, in the forest-dwelling stage of life, a Hindu left their family home to renounce the world and social connections (Kaelber, 2004). By drawing on a cultural ideal, the ashram-like old-age homes leveraged the preoccupation with self-expression common in post-industrial economies.

The value modernization framework would suggest "self-expression" provides only the general direction of an attitude toward the elderly. Cultural context, unique historical circumstances, and the actions and choices of individuals would create the actual attitudes.

What Do You Owe Your Parents? Perspectives from Value Modernization

The value modernization framework suggested a gradual shift in stereotypes of the elderly, including stereotypes related to what the elderly "deserve" (and conversely what younger members of society "owe" them). At very low levels of economic development, consistent with pre-literate tribes, the elderly were at a distinct disadvantage because they were less likely to be able to contribute to the physical survival of the society. In such a society, we might have owed our parents respect for their accumulated knowledge, but we were less likely to be able to provide them physical support in extremely trying circumstances.

At somewhat higher levels of economic development, we would have expected reverse ageism, which favored the elderly over the young. According to this logic, we owed respect and even obedience to our parents on account of their accumulated wisdom. We did not owe them financial support, for the simple reason that societies in which traditional authority was valued express these values by favoring the elderly in other ways.

Higher levels of economic development typically eroded traditional authority, due to a combination of factors including the development of mass education and an emphasis on secular or rational authority. However, they also created gaps in the financial support of the elderly that were only later filled by public pensions and other programs. Filial responsibility laws were an outgrowth of this gap, drawing directly on the earlier parish poor relief system. English church parishes maintained financial support for the elderly whom they deemed as deserving of charity. Disabled workmen, widows, and other older adults without substantial financial resources could expect to transition to partial or complete dependence on the poor relief system, but parish councils decided whether and how much each individual received. Records from English parishes in the 1600s indicated that older adults who behaved in ways that ran counter to this stereotype, such as by treating their pensions as entitlements rather than acts of charity, could be denied aid. Another major factor in how much an older adult received from the parish was whether they had children or other relatives who could afford to provide partial or full support (Botelho, 2004). The assumption that children owed their parents financial support became enshrined in later systems, including in the filial support laws. The compassionate ageism that grew out of a combination of increased economic need and decreased traditional authority indicated that while we owed our parents financial support, we no longer owed them respect for wisdom or obedience. While more recent developments provided greater government support for the elderly in the form of public pensions and health care, the filial support laws remained on the books in many states.

The value modernization framework suggests an additional shift: the shift toward self-expression or self-actualization that accompanies the development of service industries. The form that self-expression takes can differ dramatically by culture and social group. In coming years, ageism may shift to encompass the idea that the elderly have a unique opportunity to express or actualize themselves during the years we once thought of as retirement years, and perhaps even a moral responsibility to do so. Most of these activities are individual quests, but in some cases, they require substantial financial resources to allow the elderly person to participate. For instance, on the level of individual families, the ashram-like old-age homes require the older adults or their adult children to pay for the extensive services that make a forest retreat possible. On a public policy level, advocates of **productive aging** would ideally want government policies to encourage older adults to remain in socially productive activities such as volunteering, paid work, and care giving, not only for their contributions to society as a whole but also as a way to help older adults remain active and fulfilled in later life (Morrow-Howell, Gonzales, Matz-Costa, & Greenfield, 2015). In post-industrial economies, we might begin to wonder whether the elderly deserve the best chances possible to pursue self-expression and self-actualization in later life, and whether their children or society as a whole has a responsibility to support those pursuits.

Conclusion

In this chapter, we have suggested that we can partly understand ageism in terms of economic development, but that link is imperfect. We observed a few general trends, including the authority and well-being shifts, that helped to account for commonalities between cultures at similar levels of economic development. Overall, we have argued that economic development creates signposts for ageism, but cultures take unique pathways.

Discussion Questions

1 What do you owe your parents? Should filial responsibility laws that require adult children to support their parents be enforced, and if so, do the characteristics and behaviors of the elderly parents and the children matter?

2   Even positive stereotypes have downsides. Traditional authority stereotypes can translate to prejudice against the young (reverse ageism), while compassionate ageism stereotypes depict the elderly as incompetent and frail. What downsides might self-expression stereotypes have for the elderly or for others?
3   Consider the empty quadrant in Figure 2.1 (high self-expression, high traditional values). Under what conditions might a culture end up in this quadrant? The United States (along with some similar cultures) is a "deviant" case that falls into this quadrant. What are some possible explanations for the unusually high traditional values in the United States, relative to its level of development?

3 Framing Ageism
The Well-Educated Barista in Historical Perspective

Even after the end of the Great Recession, media outlets continued to raise the alarm about the number of college graduates who were underemployed, working in jobs far beneath their educational credentials. A shocking number of liberal-arts majors, the media reported, worked as baristas in coffee shops or as clerks in stores rather than in jobs that required a college education. After taking on tens of thousands of dollars in college debt, they spent most of their meagre pay on their student loans and were losing hope that they would find good jobs. One article in the *Wall Street Journal* welcomed us to the "well-educated-barista economy" (Galston, 2014), an economy in which college just didn't pay off financially.

Stories of older Americans working longer contrasted with those of younger workers who could not find good jobs, causing many to ask whether older workers who stayed in the labor force longer squeezed out the young. At the time the recession began, the average retirement age had been increasing for over a decade, due in part to reduced disincentives to work in the form of Social Security reforms, a shift away from physically demanding work, and better average health, coupled with a decreased financial readiness for retirement (Rutledge, Gillis, & Webb, 2015). In 2013, over half of households age 55 or older had less than $25,000 saved for retirement (United States Government Accountability Office, 2015), contributing to a steady increase in the average retirement ages of both men and women. While inadequate retirement savings were due in large part to long-term trends, the sharp decreases in housing equity and stock prices during the recession put the financial neediness of older workers into the spotlight.

Into this context, many people began to view good jobs as a scarce resource that might be unfairly distributed between the old and young. Historically, the question of whether some groups (such as immigrants or women) take jobs from other groups (such as native-born Americans or men) recurs, particularly in times of high unemployment. The "well-educated baristas" versus "older workers" issue is another variant of the same question (Munnell & Wu, 2013), one that will likely continue to get attention as college costs continue to rise. The implicit question many of these media accounts ask is "How can we prevent older adults from crowding the young out of the good jobs?" In this chapter, we propose that before we begin to find the *answer*, we need to understand stereotype content that underpins the *question*.

As discussed in Chapter 1, most theories of ageism explain stereotype processes, which are stable over time and context, rather than stereotype content. And even those which deal with stereotype content (such as Fiske et al., 1999) generally posit a stereotype that changes little over time and context. In Chapter 2, we proposed a framework for linking economic development to ageism, but emphasized that culture also played a role. In this chapter, we argue that what we consider the content of ageism is also partly a matter of the success or failure of the dominant ageism **frame**, the "central organizing idea or story line that provides meaning to an unfolding strip of events" (Gamson & Modigliani, 1987, p. 143) in organizing our everyday experiences. While the underlying reasons for bias against the aged (the processes of ageism, level of economic development, and culture) may be relatively consistent, much of the content of that bias changes depending on how frames succeed or fail in historical content.

We begin by outlining several key concepts of frame analysis. We then use these concepts to trace the history of ageism in the United States from 1900 to the present with an emphasis on three different frames: compassionate ageism, generational equity, and generational interdependence. We take another look at the "well-educated-barista economy" from the perspective of each of these frames, showing how we can find or exclude real-world evidence to support each frame, suggesting what issues each frame would identify based on that evidence, and discussing their prescriptive implications—what we as a society *should* do about underemployment among new college graduates.

Frame Analysis: The Limits of Human Rationality

Frame analysis, a research method that focuses on the frames that give meaning to everyday experience, has roots in sociology (Goffman, 1974), psychology and behavioral economics (Tversky & Kahneman, 1981), and media and social movement studies (Gamson & Modigliani, 1987). From one perspective, the concept of frames bears a strong resemblance to Allport's (1979) theory of prejudice. The human mind needs frames to organize experience and make it meaningful. But frame analysis places far more emphasis on how individuals enact, build on, and transform these frames. Because frames influence how people see and react to the world, individuals and organizations have a vested interest in promoting or undermining certain frames. Below, we (1) discuss frames as organizers of everyday experience and then (2) highlight the ways in which frames can fail, collapse, or adapt. As you read, consider what frames or basic assumptions might explain our concern about older adults taking good jobs from younger adults.

Frames as Organizers of Everyday Experience

One of the best-known articulations of framing theory, Erving Goffman's (1974) *Frame Analysis* detailed how human beings made sense of the world using a complex set of frames, groups of rules, and premises that gave meaning to experiences that would otherwise be meaningless. Typically, more than one frame was relevant to any given situation, because some of these frames guided perceptions of natural occurrences while others guided perceptions of social occurrences. To plan to wear rainboots and raincoats in April, we needed both a natural framework ("It rained more in the spring because of seasonal weather patterns") and a social framework ("We needed to wear clothing"). Goffman referred to these fundamental frames as **primary frames**, the sets of rules and premises so embedded in our worldview that they seem impervious to change. For instance, if you believe in scientific explanations of the weather, it is unlikely that you would attribute spring rains to tribal gods rather than weather patterns. Resting on a foundation of primary frames, a set of **secondary frames** guided our specific understandings and actions, such as what type of raingear to wear.

Reversals of Preference

Because the same strip of experience can have entirely different meanings depending on what we consider relevant evidence (e.g., whether season matters to the likelihood of rain), different framing can cause sharp **preference reversals**, in which the relative frequency of preferences changes based on non-rational criteria. In everyday experience, this typically happens with secondary frames. The type of raincoat you want to wear can easily change with fashion, but your view of the natural causes of weather patterns probably will not. At some point, we remove secondary frames so far from the original primary frames that they resemble houses of cards, propped up by only slight resemblances to the primary frame.

In some cases, such as the precise language used to frame issues, people may not even notice the importance of the secondary frame. For instance, in one classic experiment, psychologists Amos Tversky and Daniel Kahneman (1981) asked a group of about 150 people to make a difficult hypothetical decision. Each person needed to decide between two programs designed to combat a rare disease that scientists projected would kill 600 people. Program A would save 200 people. Program B was riskier, with a one-third chance of saving 600 people and a two-thirds chance of saving no one. Over 70 percent of the participants, when choosing between the sure results from Program A and the risky results from Program B, chose Program A. Tversky and Kahneman asked a second group of over 150 respondents to choose between Programs C and D. If the government adopted Program C, 400 people would die. If the government adopted Program D, there was a one-third chance that no one would die, but a two-thirds chance that 600 people would die. When choosing between the guaranteed results from Program C and the risky results from Program D, almost 80 percent of respondents chose Program D.

Since you can see both sets of programs, you likely notice that Programs A and C are identical, as are Programs B and D—except for the language that frames them. The choices people make differ dramatically depending on the framing of the program descriptions. The "disease" experiment provides a dramatic example of the power of secondary frames. Even frames that we might easily overlook, such as the precise language used to describe a program, can have the power to cause people to reverse their decisions.

Building Frames

Unlike the specific secondary frames in the experiment described above, the primary natural and social frames provide very little direct guidance for understanding complex issues. In the example of raincoats in the spring, we know it is likely to rain and that we need to wear clothing, but it takes other frames to determine what *type* of clothing is appropriate. Frame analysis emphasizes the role of human agency in getting from the most fundamental to the least fundamental frames.

Goffman (1974) refers to additional frames that we layer on top of primary frames as "laminations," and argues that we continually use keys to let us know when to "put on" or "take off" laminations. For instance, consider a wrestling show: a television program (lamination 3) that depicts an edited version of a dramatization (lamination 2) of a sport (lamination 1) based on a fight (primary frame). With each lamination, the meaning of the frame changes, and we use keys (or social cues) to indicate where the frames begin and end. Normally we would stop a fight from occurring, but when we know it is a sport, an entirely different set of rules applies. Over time, laminations become relatively stable secondary frames in themselves, but they almost always remain more vulnerable than the primary frames on which they rest.

The Dangerous Lives of Secondary Frames

Secondary frames draw strength from primary frames, but the connection between primary and secondary frames becomes increasingly tenuous with each layer added. In part, this is because more than one secondary framing of our experiences can appear to "make sense": to line up with reality, to resonate with our most deeply held values, and to draw on key aspects of primary frames. Consequently, secondary frames are precarious, and can be unseated much more easily than primary frames.

A first source of danger to secondary frames comes from the evidence of the world itself. **Individual frame breaks**—when people step outside of the rules and expectations of a frame—occur by accident, such as a runway model falling down during a fashion show, or as part of a performance or joke. People can also break frame intentionally. Cheating at cards is a frame break because it violates the rules of the game. We expect a certain amount of deviance or rule breaking for almost any frame. However, when frame breaks become both public and numerous, they throw the value of the frame as a way to organize experience into question.

Second, frames can collapse in the face of competing frames that either are—or appear to be—better ways of organizing experience. In the political realm, the way that various social movements and political groups frame issues can influence how we perceive and react to them. Famously, manuals by pollster Frank Luntz and cognitive linguist George Lakoff have told conservatives and liberals, respectively, how to successfully frame campaign messages (Scheufele & Tewksbury, 2007). Other literature, such as Gamson and Modigliani (1989), looks at the relationship between frames promoted in the media and public opinion. Individuals and organizations actively make, challenge, and remake secondary frames, with tangible effects on the outcomes of various issues.

Framing Ageism: The United States, 1900 to Present

Many of the secondary frames that we have described (raincoat fashions, wrestling shows) are so far removed from their primary frames (weather patterns, fights) that they are very fragile. Consider, for instance, how easily different designers can change our definition of fashionable clothing. The deeper and more fundamental (the more "primary") a frame is, the less likely it is to collapse, even in the face of contrary evidence. We are likely to respond instead by reframing our experiences using aspects of the original frame, but in slightly different ways. Below, we outline the way that ageism has been framed and reframed from approximately 1900 to the present day in the United States, paying particular attention to the role of compassionate ageism in the development of the old-age welfare state and to the development of alternative frames in the later generational equity debate.

Compassionate Ageism and the Old-Age Welfare State

What sociologist Gøsta Esping-Andersen (1999) terms **homo liberalismus** (liberal man) is one of the most basic and widely held social frames in the United States. Like *homo economicus* (economic man), the unrealistic hero of so many economic theories, *homo liberalismus* connects the value of individualism to everyday experience by assuming that a person has the right, and often the responsibility, to pursue their own self-interest. Within this frame, we would view a person who refuses to improve their economic lot in life as an object of derision and censure. But *homo liberalismus* is not purely individualistic. It combines the pursuit of self-interest with a propensity to be "generous, even altruistic" (Esping-Andersen, 1999, p. 171) as long as governments or other institutions do not dictate that generosity. This frame, as a way of understanding responsibilities to vulnerable populations, emphasizes voluntary acts of kindness and charity, while remaining resistant to the compulsory programs associated with activist governments. We can view many of the frames of American culture, such as frames for understanding poverty, as secondary frames resting on this more basic frame. Among these, compassionate ageism, which defines the elderly as poor and frail, and hence deserving of help and pity because they cannot pursue their own self-interests in the market, has one of the longest histories (Binstock, 1983). In its original incarnation—or at least the incarnation that dominated at the beginning of the twentieth century—compassionate ageism emphasized that the elderly were deserving of aid, but without any expectation that such aid would come from government activism. The help that the elderly received should come from their families or voluntary benefactors instead. Even as **public pension programs**, which allotted government payments to the elderly, became commonplace in Europe, responsibility for the elderly remained in individual hands in the United States (Binstock, 2010). For decades into the twentieth century, compassionate ageism carried with it an unspoken resistance to government activism on behalf of the elderly that seemed almost unshakeable.

The dire consequences of the Great Depression, though, constituted a **collective frame break**. The number of deviants from the accepted social frame, which emphasized self-reliance, a lack of government activism, and voluntary charity for deserving groups, exploded. By throwing laissez-faire capitalism into a stark and unflattering light, the Depression convinced many Americans that self-reliance alone was a flawed ideal. Into this context, a more activist government introduced a wide range of New Deal programs aimed to help various populations such as young unemployed men (e.g., the Civilian Conservation Corps) and the elderly (e.g., Social Security). Many of the New Deal programs did not survive the end of the Great Depression. They targeted groups that the public saw as temporarily distressed rather than in need of permanent help (McNamara, Sano, & Williamson, 2012), particularly in light of the United States' entry into World War II and the subsequent economic boom.

The programs targeted toward the elderly met a very different fate. Due to the influence of the compassionate ageism frame, Americans viewed the elderly as *permanently* in need and deserving of help. The enactment of Social Security in 1935 marked the beginning of an old-age welfare state which, while limited compared to its counterparts in many European countries, continued to expand over the next four decades (Hudson, 1978). Later programs included Medicare and Medicaid (1965), which provided health insurance to most older Americans; the Older Americans Act, which provided services to elders (1965); the Age Discrimination in Employment Act, aimed to protect older workers from discrimination (1967); the Age Discrimination Act (1975), which protected older adults from discrimination in programs receiving federal funding; the Employee Retirement Income Security Act (1974), which regulated pension programs, and the Research on Aging Act (1974), which established the National Institute on Aging (Binstock, 2010). Americans had reframed compassionate ageism to allow for more government activism, with positive material consequences for the elderly. The increased spending led to steep declines in old-age poverty and increased financial well-being of older adults (Binstock, 2010). The Great Depression constituted a collective frame break, in which the challenge to a frame came primarily from everyday experience, without which proponents of government activism could not have instituted these policies.

Competing Frames: The Generational Equity Debate

A second major reframing occurred in the 1980s. A short-term Social Security funding shortfall and the subsequent adoption of the 1983 Social Security Amendments drew public attention to the large proportion of the federal budget spent on old-age programs (Williamson & Rhodes, 2011). The funding shortfall, by itself, was not nearly as compelling a collective event as the Great Depression, but instead created an opportunity for reframing by calling into question the neediness of the elderly. It triggered the **generational equity debate**, a debate between two competing frames: generational equity and generational interdependence.

The Generational Equity Frame

Previous literature has argued that the **generational equity frame**, which focused attention on the extent to which the elderly might be getting more than their fair share at the expense of children and younger adults (Williamson & Watts-Roy, 2009), came into public discourse as part of the larger strategy of a loose coalition of conservative organizations, journalists, and foundations. In the years following the 1983 Social Security Amendment, Senator David Durenberger, with funding from conservative foundations and businesses, founded Americans for Generational Equity (AGE) (Binstock, 1999; Quadagno, 1989). Other advocates of the generational equity frame included journalists such as William F. Buckley, Jr. and organizations such as the Cato Institute and the Olin Foundation (Williamson, McNamara, & Howling, 2003), for whom generational equity was part of a larger push away from activist government rather than the primary issue. In the words of journalist Henry Fairlie's (1988) well-known article, the proponents of the generational equity frame implied that the elderly were "greedy geezers."

On a public policy level, the generational equity frame focused attention on certain aspects of our collective experience while neglecting others. For example, AGE and other advocates of the generational equity frame highlighted demographer Samuel Preston's (1984) observation that the economic conditions of the elderly had improved while those of children had deteriorated (McNamara et al., 2012). All else being equal, he observed, the continued decline in the proportion of the population under age 15 would have translated into more funding available per child. At the same time, if spending on programs for the elderly remained the same overall, as the proportion of the elderly population grew, less assistance would be available per elderly person. The fact that the financial status of the elderly had instead improved while that of children had deteriorated resulted partly from a political decision-making process that approved large transfers from working-age adults to the elderly in the form of taxes. Preston argued that because working-age adults were the primary supporters of children, transfers toward the elderly were also in a sense transfers away from children.

Over time, the generational equity frame continued to evolve. Rather than focusing only on Social Security and Medicare spending, it spilled over to other programs such as age-based subsidized housing (Williamson & Rhodes, 2011). For instance, in the early 1990s, economists Alan Auerbach, Jagadeesh Gokhale, and Lawrence Kotlikoff (1991) developed **generational accounting**, which aimed to calculate a **lifetime net tax rate** for each generation: what they would pay in taxes minus the government transfers that they could expect to receive under various assumptions. As shown in Figure 3.1, this approach highlighted the greater lifetime tax burdens on younger generations as compared to older generations. In 2012, over the course of his lifetime, a 20-year-old man would have expected to pay about 271,000 dollars more in taxes than they received as transfers. Conversely, a 70-year-old man would have expected to receive about 285,000 dollars more in government transfers than he paid in taxes. The authors suggested that focusing on the lifetime net tax rate rather than spending at any given

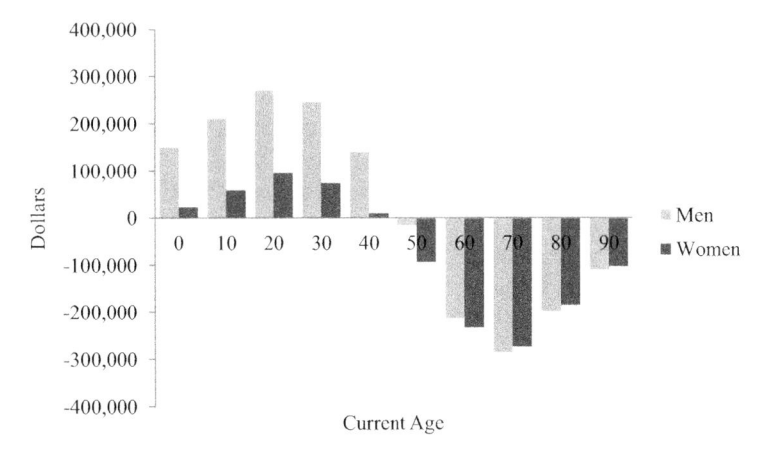

Figure 3.1 Lifetime generational accounts using generational accounting methods
Note: Based on public policy assumptions in 2012
Source: Gokhale, 2012

time would allow us to assess the equitability of various proposals to change Social Security, Medicare, and other government programs more fairly. Generational accounting, which was in many ways a budgetary manifestation of the generational equity frame, never gained precedence over more traditional methods of evaluating the costs and benefits of federal programs. However, it continued to influence our thinking and ensured that the public considered equity between generations as "an issue" or even "the issue" when considering the federal budget.

Much of the generational equity frame's success comes from its link to fairness or justice. American culture combines high individualism, as manifest in the original incarnation of compassionate ageism, with relatively low **power distance**, a term social psychologist Hofstede and his colleagues (Hofstede, Hofstede, & Minkov, 1993) use to describe the extent to which cultures expect and accept inequalities. Cultures with high power distance accept a power differential between those at the higher and lower ends of the social hierarchy. Cultures with low power distance resist inequalities or reframe them to include a base element of equality or equity. In the case of the United States, high individualism combined with lower power distance results in a characteristic emphasis on equity, fairness, or justice. The prevailing view is that, ideally, people can earn different outcomes through their own efforts, but these outcomes should be equitably distributed according to effort.

The Generational Interdependence Frame

Beginning in the 1990s, the competing **generational interdependence frame**—which emphasized the ways in which generations and age cohorts were interdependent rather than competing or conflicting (Beard & Williamson 2004)—arose as a response to both compassionate ageism and generational equity. This frame included two distinct facets. First, the generational interdependence frame highlighted the common interests of generations (Kingson, Hirshorn, & Cornman, 1986). For instance, they noted that the deterioration in the financial status of children stemmed from structural changes such as increasing proportions of single-parent households and policy changes such as reductions in federal spending on the poor, rather than from spending on the elderly. Second, the generational interdependence frame emphasized the wide variation in the characteristics of the elderly (Williamson et al., 2003). While there might be "greedy geezers" and "doddering but dear" old ladies, proponents of this frame argued, there was as much or more variation among the elderly as among other age group.

The two frames looked at the same strips of experience, but drew our attention to entire different aspects of those experiences. For instance, despite the importance of Preston's (1984) data to proponents of the generational equity frame, he acknowledged that structural changes were partly responsible for the deteriorating status of children, a key argument of the generational interdependence frame. Given that they began with the same data, the relative lack of success of the generational interdependence frame in guiding policy discourse highlights the importance of the foundational frame. One major reason that the generational interdependence frame met with cultural resistance was that it drew on obligations to community (Williamson et al., 2003). While the emphasis on charity and altruism might be a strong element of Hofstede's *homo liberalismus* and its secondary frames such as compassionate ageism, it was subordinate to individualism. Consequently, generational interdependence, regardless of how well rooted in fact its claims might be, stood on softer cultural ground than generational interdependence.

Framing the "Well-Educated-Barista Economy"

Above, we highlight three possible frames for understanding the elderly: compassionate ageism, since the 1930s including an acceptance of government activism; generational equity, with an emphasis on fairness across generations; and generational interdependence, with a focus on the ways in which people of different ages are interconnected. Below, we both apply each of these frames to the "well-educated-barista economy." As our earlier discussion of frame analysis indicates, frames (1) draw our attention to particular pieces of *evidence* while neglecting information; (2) suggest what the *real issues* are, and hence what the relevant *questions* are; and (3) carry prescriptions about what we *should* do for and about social issues. Below, we highlight each of these issues in relation to the three frames.

Compassionate Ageism: The Specter of Old-Age Poverty

Evidence

The compassionate ageism frame focuses our attention on the lack of retirement readiness among older adults. Older workers today are less financially prepared to retire, as compared to those who have reached retirement age in the immediately preceding decades. Some estimates indicate that up to a third of workers approaching the age of retirement (ages 55 to 64) would live in poverty or near poverty in old age, if they relied only on their retirement savings and assets (Saad-Lessler, Ghilarducci, & Bahn, 2015). While Social Security helps to bring older adults further above the poverty line, even counting government transfers about 45 percent of households aged 50 to 59 are at risk of being unable to maintain their standard of living in retirement (Munnell, Hou, & Webb, 2014). If older adults work a few years longer while they are able to do so, it could help them to maintain sufficient standards of living later in life.

Issue, Question, Prescription

Compassionate ageism draws our attention to the specter of poverty in old age. The real *issue* is the circumstances that have increased the odds that older adults will need to work longer for financial reasons, even if they do not want to do so. The primary *question* to ask about the well-educated-barista economy is, "How can we improve retirement readiness so older adults can afford to retire, freeing up jobs for the young?" To the extent that older adults continue to work because of inadequate savings, we *should* take action to ensure retirement readiness.

Generational Equity: No Bright Beginnings

Evidence

The generational equity framework focuses on evidence of scarce resources, the idea that there are not enough resources to provide for all social groups. For instance, the stagnation and decline of real wages, combined with growing wage inequality (Autor, Katz, & Kearney, 2008), may have allowed for this frame to take root in the 1980s and, more recently, the Great Recession has similarly fed the idea that there are not enough resources to provide for all social groups (Edsall 2012). Nowhere is this more obvious than in the discussions of underemployment among young college-educated adults. According to this logic, there are simply not enough "good jobs" to go around and, given the staggering increases in college costs, new college graduates deserve a chance at those jobs. As shown in Figure 3.2, the cost of tuition, fees, room, and board at a four-year college has more than doubled over the past 20 years, even adjusting for inflation. Consequently, new college graduates do not face the same bright beginnings as earlier generations. And, as Peter Cappelli (2015) points out, despite overwhelming evidence that college pays off in general, it doesn't pay off for everyone. At the extreme, about 45 percent of recent college graduates are underemployed (Abel & Deitz, 2016), working in jobs that they do not need a four-year degree to do.

Issue, Question, Prescription

According to the generational equity frame, the real *issue* is the extent to which scarce resources, including good jobs, are being unfairly or unfairly allocated across generations. There is only so much to go around, so the interests of older adults must be balanced against the interests of younger adults. The primary *question* that this frame asks about the well-educated barista is the one with which we started this chapter: "How can we prevent older adults from crowding the young out of the good jobs?" To the extent that younger adults are especially disadvantaged because of college loans, we

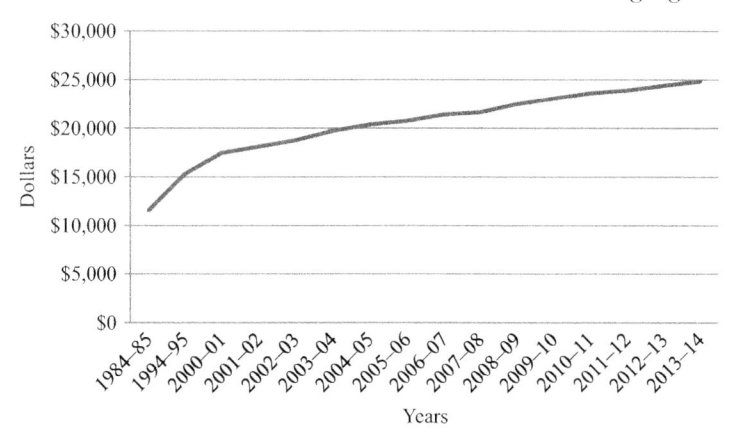

Figure 3.2 Cost of four-year college degree in 2014–15 dollars
Note: Includes both public and private institutions
Source: U.S. Department of Education, National Center for Education Statistics. (2016). Digest of Education Statistics, 2015 (NCES 2016–014), chapter 3

should provide more policies to help them break into the labor market sooner and fewer policies to encourage older adults to remain in the labor market longer.

Generational Interdependence: We're All in This Together

Evidence

The generational interdependence frame highlights evidence indicating that generations are interconnected. This frame would focus first on how the troubles of both new college graduates and near retirees spring from what political scientist Jacob Hacker (2006) calls the **great risk shift**, "the massive transfer of economic risk from broad structures of insurance, including those sponsored by the corporate sector as well as by government, onto the fragile balance sheets of American families" (p. 6). The rise of defined contribution pension plans, which unlike defined benefit pension plans do not provide a fixed monetary benefit in retirement and rely largely on employee contributions, has shifted financial risk away from corporations and onto older workers (Hacker, 2011). The rapid increase in college costs, and the consequent growth in student loan balances, represents another major force driving risk shifts (Glater, 2015).

Issue, Question, Prescription

According to the generational interdependence frame, the real *issue* is the extent to which, through political and economic changes, risk has shifted from large collectives (the government, employers) to families and individuals. This only exacerbates the necessity for families to rely on each other across generations for financial and social support. Given the financial stressors across the life course, it is perhaps not surprising that the proportion of multigenerational households continues to rise as younger and older adults pool resources (see Figure 3.3). The primary *question* to ask about the well-educated-barista economy is, "How can we strengthen the social safety net so that it better protects families and individuals of all ages from economic risks?" For younger adults, such measures *should* include strengthening tuition-forgiveness programs. For older adults, measures *should* include improvements to defined contribution pensions, such as automatic enrollment or automatic increases in contributions over time.

Just the Facts? The Lump of Labor

Above, we have discussed three very different ways to understand the "well-educated-barista economy," motivated by three different frames: compassionate ageism, generational equity, and generational interdependence. You have learned that these frames developed under diverse historical conditions, and that they not only help us to identify evidence, they also cause us to downplay or ignore other information. You might come to the conclusion that the real problem is "all frame, no substance" and wonder what the facts say about this issue.

We chose the well-educated barista issue as an example of framing for a very specific reason: it is widely considered a *non*-issue in the academic

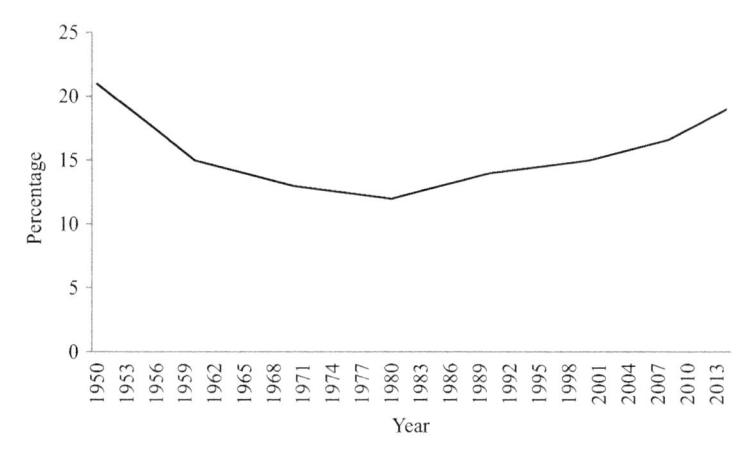

Figure 3.3 Percentage of American population living in a multigenerational household
Note: Includes those living in households with (a) at least two adult generations or (b) grandchildren and grandparents
Source: Pew Research Center, 2016

literature. The majority of labor economists consider the idea that some workers crowd out other workers a mirage, often derisively labeled the **lump of labor fallacy**. The fallacy, which assumes that there is a certain amount of work to be done and that we need to divide jobs up equitably, serves as an unspoken justification for policy agendas ranging from immigration restriction (to prevent immigrants from "taking the jobs" of native-born citizens) to limiting the length of the work week (to decrease unemployment by spreading the number of hours to be worked around more people). This chapter's initial question relies on the same kind of zero-sum thinking. In reality, there is no fixed "pie" divided between the old and young. The economy can grow or shrink depending on various opportunities and constraint (Munnell & Wu, 2013). Perhaps the biggest reason that the lump of labor fallacy never quite dies is that the evidence of our everyday lives can seem to contradict it We may meet an older worker who does not retire, preventing younger workers from moving up in a company. We may know a college-educated barista who cannot land a job in the fields for which he or she studied. We may feel concern for an older person who is financially unsettled because they had to retire earlier than they otherwise would have. Frames, by helping us to make sense of everyday experience, can have more power than most objective data.

Conclusion

In this chapter, we have argued that we can understand the history of ageism in the United States, particularly since the Great Depression, as a history of frames. Frame analysis illuminates how frames organize our everyday experience, and also how they can become battlegrounds through which organizations and individual actors promote their preferred way of spotting relevant evidence, identifying the key issues, proposing questions, and guiding our actions, as in the example of the well-educated barista.

Discussion Questions

1 Some authors have proposed that another possible frame, one rooted in theories of ageism, could be useful in understanding these issues: the cumulative inequality frame, which highlights the ways in which economic and social advantage accumulate over time (Beard & Williamson, 2016). Using the well-educated-barista issue, try to identify the (a) real-world evidence; (b) the "real issue"; and (c) the "key question" that the cumulative inequality frame would highlight.
2 The "great risk shift" is real, but is it right? Should the responsibility and control of saving for retirement be primarily on the individual? How about the responsibility for paying for college? If you think risk for retirement but not education should be individual (or vice versa), why?

4 Ageism at the Crossroads
Intersectionality and the Life Course

Consider the movies you have seen lately. How old are the actors and actresses who receive top billing in those movies? The top-billed actors and actresses typically have the most screen time and the most important roles. With some exceptions, you will probably find that more actors than actresses receive top billing, and that the actresses whose names do appear at the top of movie credits are substantially younger than the actors from the same movies.

In the popular press, the widespread availability of online databases provides continued evidence of gendered ageism in the film industry. A 2015 *Time Magazine* analysis reports that, in an analysis of 6,000 actors and actresses, the average number of roles that men receive peaks at about five roles per year around age 46, and then gradually declines. The average number of roles that women receive peaks at about four roles per year at age 30, then sharply declines (Wilson, 2015). Similarly, a census of 8,000 screenplays, on the popular website Polygraph (2016), indicates that the percentage of movie dialogue available to women decreases as they age, while that available to men increases. Academic research points to the same relationship between age, gender, and success in Hollywood. One analysis of the salaries of Hollywood's top movie stars finds that on average actors' market values increase until age 51 then stabilize, while actresses' market values increase until age 34 then decrease (De Pater, Judge, & Scott, 2014). In terms of number of roles, salaries, and dialogue available to them, most actresses are "over the hill" at the age of 30 or 35. Actresses that remain in demand, receive top salaries, and get leading roles into their 50s, 60s, and beyond are few in number, when compared to actors who are able to do the same.

We might be tempted to call Hollywood ageist, but the story isn't that simple. The film industry does not subject men to the same level of ageism as women. Further, some acclaimed actresses do defy the general trend, and are more popular and celebrated as they age. We might conclude from the example of aging movie actresses that ageism interacts with other forms of prejudice, such as prejudice based on gender, race, ethnicity, and sexual orientation. But the exact mechanisms through which ageism and other forms of diversity interact are less than straightforward.

In this chapter, we present a set of complementary perspectives that focus on the overlapping nature of prejudice and discrimination. We argue that what we typically think of as "ageism" combines three distinct components: (1) a general stereotype of the aged; (2) a set of specific "ageisms" based on **intersectionality**, the interconnections between perceptions and experiences of different social categories, such as race and ethnicity, gender, age, and sexual orientation; and (3) the long-term effects of ageism over the **life course**, the sequence of events and roles that individuals enact over the course of their lives (Elder, 1994). Figure 4.1 maps these approaches. Throughout this chapter, we return to the question of aging actresses to evaluate which perspective on ageism and diversity, if any, might explain their declining status over time in film.

Compassionate Ageism and Its Challengers

At any given time, one or more general stereotypes of the elderly vies for cultural dominance. At least since the Industrial Revolution, Western culture's emphasis on individualism and youth has promoted a stereotype that the elderly are incompetent, meaning they are frail and needing assistance, and warm, meaning they are likeable and deserving of help (Cuddy & Fiske, 2002). Binstock (1983) referred to this general stereotype as "compassionate ageism," while Cuddy and Fiske (2002) called it a paternalistic stereotype. As we discussed in Chapter 3, this

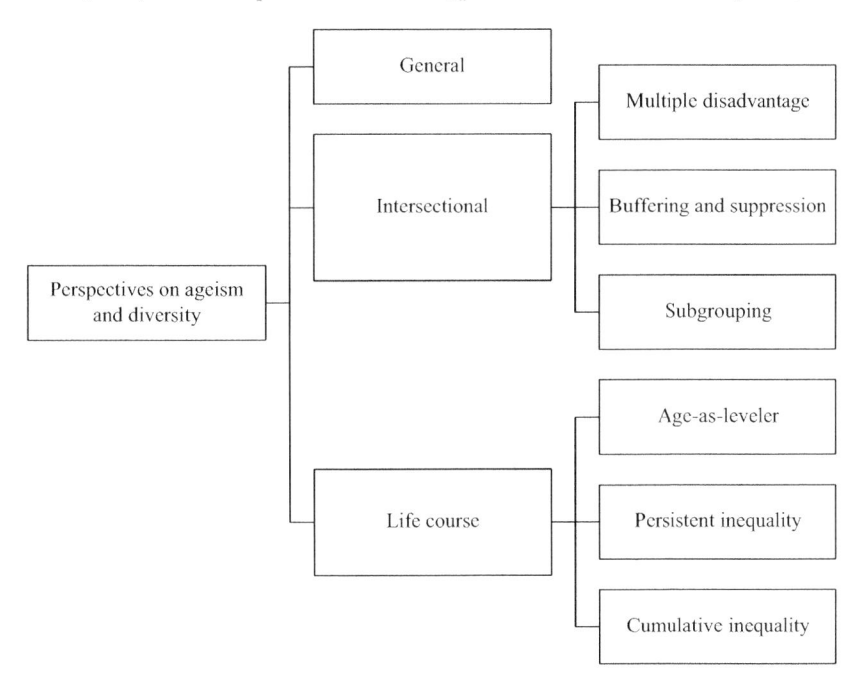

Figure 4.1 Perspectives on ageism and diversity

stereotype, however, competes with other views of the elderly, such as the "greedy geezer" stereotype, which views the elderly as taking more than their fair share of resources at the expense of the young (Fairlie, 1988). These general approaches to ageism present widely divergent and competing views of the elderly. However, they also each present a relatively monolithic or general stereotype, a stereotype that concerns the elderly as a whole.

The trouble with general stereotypes, whether positive or negative, is that they cannot fully explain how ageism operates in real life. For instance, actresses seem to suffer from ageism, receiving fewer roles as they age. Based on what you have learned in Chapter 1, you might hypothesize, using Cuddy and Fiske's (2002) stereotype content model, that, since most people consider movie stars successful (or competent), we avoid movies starring the elderly (generally viewed as incompetent). Or, using terror management theory, you might hypothesize that people fear the elderly because they represent death, causing them to avoid movies that feature older people prominently. Both explanations seem to explain the decrease in roles, pay, and prominence of actresses as they age, but do little to explain why the same does not occur for actors.

The Intersectionality of Prejudice

We argue here that many of the key reasons that aging actors fare better than aging actresses are related to intersectionality. You probably already recognize intersectionality in daily life. For instance, consider your stereotype of the elderly. If you are like most people today, you consider elderly people in general to be likeable. You might pity them for being frail, considering them deserving of help and protection. Now imagine a specific elderly person that you know and consider whether the general elderly stereotype applies to them. You will probably discover that general stereotypes seldom fit specific individuals well. In addition to being elderly, that person is male or female, of a particular race and ethnicity, and of a specific sexual orientation. Real people are resistant to such general categories as "the elderly" not only because of individual idiosyncrasies, but also because they fit into numerous other social categories.

Intersectionality means that ageism, when applied in day-to-day life, typically interracts with other forms of prejudice and discrimination. However, the precise way that stereotypes interact with each other is often not straightforward. Below, we discuss three common ways in which two or more stereotypes can intersect, and then return to the question of aging actresses to suggest how each of these approaches might appear to explain their predicament.

Double Jeopardy: The Wage Gap

Among the earliest ways to look at intersectionality assumes that, for each disadvantaged status, an individual suffers from an additional burden of discrimination and prejudice. For instance, feminist and peace activist Frances

Beal's famous pamphlet *Double Jeopardy: To Be Black and Female* (1969) articulates the "double jeopardy" hypothesis clearly. She argues that the economic system of capitalism has a vested interest in creating wage discrimination, in which women command lower annual salaries than men and non-white women have the lowest salaries of all. Her example uses data from race- and gender-specific earnings. The original numbers from Beal's 1969 pamphlet are: $6,704 for white males, $4,277 for non-white males, $3,991 for white females, and $2,861 for non-white females (Bureau of Labor Statistics, cited in Beal, 1969). In her data, non-white females earn less than half of white males. Beal refers to this effect as the "**double jeopardy**" of race and gender, and more recent writers such as sociologist Deborah King (1988) refer instead to **multiple jeopardy**, the combined effects of multiple oppressive barriers, including not only racism and sexism but also discrimination based on class, sexuality, or other categories.

Double or multiple jeopardy assumes that the effects are additive, in that membership in each disadvantaged group adds to overall disadvantage. This argument seems to fit the evidence on the race-gender wage gap well, but when we apply this logic to age, the story becomes more ambiguous. Based on Beal's argument, if older adults and women are both at risk, then older women should have the lowest wages of all workers by a substantial amount. However, as shown in Figure 4.2, women earn less than men of the same age, but young men earn amounts comparable to middle-aged and older women. Instead of a simple

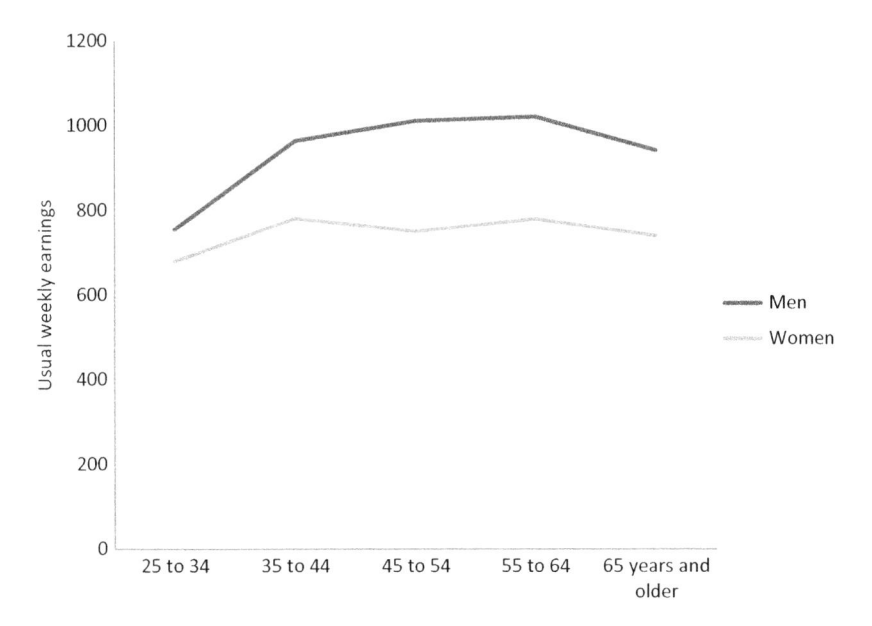

Figure 4.2 Men and women's usual weekly earnings by age (2014)
Source: Bureau of Labor Statistics, 2014, median usual weekly earnings of full-time wage and salary workers, by selected characteristics, 2014 annual averages

situation of double jeopardy, the age-gender wage gap is best understood as changing over time. The earnings of women across age look relatively "flat," and if we focus only on women's earnings, it might appear that there is no ageism present. If anything, there seems to be age equality. But keep in mind that as people age, their job tenure and job experience generally increase as well. In the absence of ageism, we would expect women employed full time to earn progressively more as they age and gain experience at least until their mid-60s, much as men do.

The difference between Beal's analysis (race-gender) and our example (age-gender) highlights both the usefulness and limitations of double jeopardy as a way of studying intersectionality. The real wage gap for women appears not in the difference between their earnings and men's earnings at any one time, but in the way that gap changes with age. Because of the nature of ageism, the jeopardy that workers find themselves in is likely to fluctuate over the course of their life and, as the example of the wage gap illustrates, the age group that is disadvantaged is not always obvious.

Stereotype Buffering: Faces of Prejudice

In the case of multiple jeopardy, the effects of prejudice are additive. But, evidence suggests that in some cases, one stereotype can buffer or protect a group from other stereotypes. We term this process **stereotype buffering**, and some of the clearest examples of such buffering comes from "facing" studies. These studies attempt to measure prejudice by asking participants to react to human faces. Most of us heavily rely on facial expressions to determine the intentions of the people around us. However, facial expressions are not always clear and unambiguous, and in those situations we interpret what we see of a person's facial expression based on other cues such as body language and ingrained prejudices.

In one study of ingrained racism, Hugenberg and Bodenhausen (2003) used a series of computer-generated faces to assess how white Americans interpreted facial affect. Using computer software, they generated two ethnically ambiguous facial structures. For each of the two facial structures, they changed only the hairstyle, hair color, and skin tone to signal that the person depicted was "black" or "white." For the resulting four faces (two black and two white), they created hostile facial expressions and happy facial expressions. Rather than present participants in the experiment with still images, they created four 16-second emotional transition movies, one for each face that showed the face gradually shifting from one expression to the other. Respondents tried to identify when each face changed expression, from happy to hostile, or from hostile to happy. Those respondents who had higher implicit prejudice against blacks, as a separate questionnaire measured it, identified black faces as becoming happy later and becoming hostile earlier.

Since then, more recent studies have applied this approach to age. For instance, Kang and Chasteen's (2009) study adapted Hugenberg and

Bodenhausen's "facial transition" approach. However, they focused on the interaction of racism and ageism, rather than on racism alone. They argued that if the double-jeopardy hypothesis held, due to the combined effects of bias against blacks and bias against the elderly, people should see elderly black men as being hostile longer than any other group. By asking individuals to react to both old and young versions of the black/white emotional transition movies, they showed that the elderly stereotype ("warm," or likeable) neutralized or buffered the hostile ("cold," or unlikeable) stereotype of black men. Respondents interpreted facial expressions as becoming hostile later and happy sooner for old black men as compared to young black men. The opposite effect occurred for old white men. Respondents considered old white men more hostile and less happy than young white men, in line with the "curmudgeon" stereotype.

These "facing" experiments show how prejudice operates at the most individual and immediate level. Our preconceptions of social categories color even our interpretations of the emotions and intentions of others. The findings of these studies also highlight the potential for one stereotype to buffer against another. Stereotype buffering involves the combined effects of two stereotypes, but unlike double or multiple jeopardy, the effects of those stereotypes can oppose each other. A positive stereotype from membership in one group buffers a group against the negative stereotype from membership in another group. In the case of Kang and Chasteen's (2009) experiment, the suppression of the hostile black male stereotype by the likeable elderly man stereotype is likely to happen gradually as a person ages.

Stereotype Subgrouping: The Power of Disconfirmers

Double jeopardy and stereotype buffering share the assumption that we can understand the effects of "combined" stereotypes (e.g., elderly black men) by understanding how the stereotypes of two or more "single" categories (e.g., the elderly, blacks, and men) interact. A different way to look at intersectionality focuses on how completely different stereotypes can arise through **subgrouping**, the process through which people recognize that there are distinctions between subgroups within a larger group. People create what we call **substereotypes**, stereotypes that apply to subgroups nested within a larger group. One famous example of a subgroup is Sojourner Truth's "A'n't I a Woman" speech. Truth's famous—although historically dubious (Painter, 1996)—observation that the stereotype of black women contrasts with that of women in general. "Dat man ober dar say dat womin needs to be helped into carriages, and lifted ober ditches, and to hab de best place everywhar. Nobody eber helps me into carriage, or ober mud-puddles, or gibs me any best place," Truth observes, "And a'n't I a woman?" (Gage, 1881).

Despite this, subgrouping is not the only way that people deal with diversity in a stereotyped group. In fact, many people tend instead to use sub*typing*, the "process by which group members who disconfirm, or are at odds with, the group stereotype are mentally clustered together" (Maurer, Park, & Rothbart, 1995). We can see subtyping as a fundamentally conservative cognitive strategy, similar to Allport's (1979) concept of cognitive "re-fencing." We build "fences" to hold prejudices about other social groups, and are prone to label individuals who do not fit that stereotype as "special cases" or "the exception that proves the rule." We then maintain existing stereotypes through subtyping by separating individuals into two groups: confirmers and disconfirmers. First, **confirmers** are those individuals who appear to fit the group stereotype. For instance, an elderly person who is kind, gentle, and frail would be a confirmer of compassionate ageism. **Disconfirmers** are individuals who appear not to fit the group stereotype. An elderly person who was hostile or in good health would be a disconfirmer of compassionate ageism. Subtyping measures both confirmers and disconfirmers against the same yardstick: an overall group stereotype.

Sub*grouping* is what happens when subtyping fails. Sometimes, we find that there are so many exceptions to our rule that the rule is no longer cognitively useful. Eventually, we realize that there is more real diversity within a group than we thought. While we might choose to throw out a stereotype entirely, it is more common to choose subgrouping as a cognitive strategy for "fencing" groups in, but with more flexibility than an overall stereotype. Subgrouping varies from subtyping because rather than separating individuals into "confirmers" (those who confirm the stereotype) and "disconfirmers" (those who disconfirm the stereotype), it acknowledges more real diversity. Clusters of individuals who do not fit the stereotype, rather than being disconfirmers or "special cases," exist within the larger **superordinate group** (Richards & Hewstone, 2001).

In one study of stereotypes of the elderly (Brewer, Dull, & Lui, 1981), the researchers asked college students to sort photographs of older adults into categories. In a first experiment, Brewer and his colleagues presented the students with a series of pictures that they then attempted to classify into categories. The students categorized them into three types: what the experimenters termed the grandmotherly type, including most female pictures; the elder statesman, including most male pictures; and the senior citizen, including both female and male pictures. In a second experiment, students sorted statements into categories to match sets of three pictures corresponding with the categories defined in the first experiment (grandmotherly, elder statesman, and senior citizen). At least 50 percent of participants who saw three grandmotherly pictures agreed that individuals from this group would be likely to have traits such as kindness and cheerfulness. At least 50 percent of participants who saw three elder statesman pictures agreed that individuals from such a group were likely to be aggressive, intelligent, conservative, dignified, neat, and authoritarian. Senior citizens, of the three subgroups, had the fewest agreed-upon traits (including only lonely and old-fashioned). When individuals saw three pictures, one from each type (grandmotherly, elder statesman, and senior citizen), there was even less consensus. That is, most of the stereotyping of the elderly occurred at the subgroup, not the superordinate, level. Participants may have had a general stereotype of "the elderly" but when confronted with real examples (whether pictures or specific individuals), they found subgrouping a more useful cognitive strategy.

Film Stars at the Intersection of Age and Gender

Consider the question of film stars from the perspective of intersectionality. At face value, the gendered ageism of the film industry might seem to be a simple case of double disadvantage. However, men are not as disadvantaged by age as women. If anything, aging benefits actors or is neutral to their success. And younger women actually have an advantage in terms of number of roles, compared to younger men (De Pater, Judge, & Scott, 2014). We might make the alternative argument that stereotype buffering is at work. Hollywood places great value on youth, and the film industry views looking "old" as unattractive to movie audiences. To the extent that we consider youthful looks less crucial to the success of men than of women, being male might buffer actors against the ageist stereotypes. Now consider the case of actresses who remain successful into their 50s, 60s, and beyond. Are they disconfirmers ("the exceptions that prove the rule") or are they a subgroup with shared characteristics that allow them to escape the negative stereotypes applied to the superordinate group ("aging actresses")?

Ageism over the Life Course

As described above, intersectionality provides at least three ways of looking at how various facets of prejudice and discrimination interact, including multiple jeopardy, stereotype buffering, and subgrouping. In this chapter, we argue that the question of ageism, age discrimination, and diversity can better be understood in terms of *intersectionality across the life course*. Consider the question of hiring. Particularly among vulnerable groups (such as racial minorities or less educated workers), a young job seeker might be unable to obtain a job, not only because of lack of job experience but because hirers perceive them as less serious and reliable. The same person, as an older adult, might also be unable to obtain a job, because despite accumulated experience, hirers view them as old-fashioned and inflexible. Because individuals from racial and ethnic minorities, women, and other vulnerable groups fare worse in the job market, ageism has the potential to disproportionately affect these vulnerable groups. That is, ageism and age discrimination occur over the course of a person's life, so that it is not possible to fully understand the intersection of ageism with other forms of prejudice (e.g., racism) without considering whether those effects persist, grow, or decrease as a person ages.

The Persistence of Inequality

One of the foundational myths of America is the idea that a person can go from "rags to riches," but the opposite is more often true. For instance, sociologist Robert Merton (1968) published a famous essay in which he found that, when two scientists published similar work, the eminent or more well-known scientist got the credit. Merton dubbed this "**The Matthew Effect**," from the Gospel of Matthew: "For unto every one that hath shall be given, and he shall have abundance: but from him that hath not shall be taken even that which he hath" (Matthew 25:29). Put in its simplest terms, "the rich get richer, the poor get poorer" because the rich are able to leverage their advantages into more advantages over time. Other writers have developed Merton's ideas into a family of closely related perspectives, referred to as **cumulative advantage, cumulative disadvantage** (Dannefer, 2003; O'Rand, 1996), and **cumulative inequality** (Ferraro and Shippee, 2009). Much of the existing research on cumulative inequality and similar perspectives has looked at tangible aspects of well-being such as health and wealth. Children "inherit" the health status and economic opportunities of their parents in a host of subtle ways. In terms of health, poor maternal nutrition and health problems in childhood go hand in hand, which in turn leads to higher likelihoods of functional limitations in adulthood (Haas & Rohlfsen, 2010). In terms of economic opportunities, children who grow up in poverty suffer from both tangible and subtle disadvantages, such as less stable family lives (O'Berg, 2003), that translate into lower levels of employment in adulthood (Ratcliffe & McKernan, 2010). Other perspectives on the life course and inequality present competing hypotheses. For instance, the **persistent inequality** hypothesis states that inequality remains relatively constant as a person ages and the **age-as-leveler hypothesis** states that inequalities tend to decrease with age (Ferraro & Farmer, 1996; Brown, O'Rand, & Adkins, 2012). But these theoretical perspectives share a focus on the role of diversity over the life course, rather than at any given point in time.

Star Presence: The Matthew Effect in Film?

Some research on aging actresses suggests that the accumulation of advantage is a key part of their decreasing status in the movie industry. When film executives view an actor or actress as a box office draw, that person is more likely to receive top billing. But in a sense this leads to the accumulation of advantage. Actors who are listed higher get more "credit" for successful movies. Those who receive lower billings gradually lose their "star power." To study this dynamic, Lincoln and Allen (2004), using data on the film industry from 1996 to 1999, calculate an actor or actress' star presence for each movie using a simple formula:

$$Star\ presence\ in\ a\ movie = \frac{1}{Ordinal\ rank\ in\ credits}$$

They also calculate an actor or actress' star presence at any given time as the mean of their star presence of all movies published in that year. An actress who is in two films, and receives top billing in one film (1/1 = 1.00) but third billing in the other film (1/3 = 0.33), has a star presence of 0.67 for that year.

Not surprisingly, controlling for factors such as whether the actors and actresses receive Oscar nominations, all but the youngest women are at a distinct disadvantage in Hollywood. Three factors may be at work. First, Western culture assumes that youth is one component of physical attractiveness, and the ageism implicit in this definition of attractiveness is nowhere more evident than in the film industry. Second, people often consider physical attractiveness more important to women than to men, meaning that actresses will typically be considered the most beautiful very early in their careers but men will be partly protected against harsh judgments as they age. This observation is consistent with stereotype buffering, in that the male stereotype partly or fully buffers actors against the ageist stereotype. Third, as Lincoln and Allen (2004) demonstrate, star presence is a self-perpetuating phenomenon. Once an actor or actress starts to lose top billing, it is harder for them to regain it, an observation consistent with the life-course perspective. As women age, their star presence suffers; and as their star presence suffers, they command lower salaries, get fewer roles, and get lower billing. Intersectionality is part of the story, but the accumulation of advantage and disadvantage over time is also an important factor. We might understand gendered ageism in Hollywood as a system in which the intersectionality of ageism and sexism accumulates over the life course.

Conclusion

In this chapter, we make the argument that, while general stereotypes of the aged do exist, to fully understand ageism and age discrimination we need to consider diversity among the aged in two distinct ways. First, we must consider the crossroads where age meets other social categories such as gender, race, ethnicity, and sexual orientation. This intersectionality can take different forms, such as multiple disadvantage, stereotype buffering, and subgrouping. Second, we need to take into account the way those intersections endure over time. Like the "star presence" in the example of Hollywood movie stars, advantage tends to accumulate over a person's life, such that the consequences of ageism are often long term.

Discussion Questions

1. Would you consider actresses who become or stay successful as they age "the exceptions that prove the rule" (subtyping) or actresses with different characteristics (subgrouping)?
2. The "facing" study implies there can be advantages to appearing older. Imagine a young adult at their first job interview out of college. Should a young adult try to appear older than their actual age when applying for a professional job? If so, how might they do this, and what might it reveal about ageism in the job market?
3. In this chapter, we purposely chose a very privileged group (movie stars who have successfully starred in widely known movies) to illustrate prejudice and discrimination. Did you have sympathy for the situation of aging actresses? Would your reaction have differed if we had illustrated the effects on a less privileged group, such as aging retail workers?

Part II

Ageism in Context

In this section, we put ageism in context by looking at how it operates in four institutions: mass media (Chapter 5), health care (Chapter 6), employment (Chapter 7), and public policy (Chapter 8). In Chapter 5, "Mass Media and the Segmentation of Ageism: A Look at Stereotypes on Facebook," we begin from the example of excoriating and infantilizing Facebook group descriptions. We propose a conceptual model for the relationship of mass media and a series of ageism "segments," including literature, television and film, magazines, and electronic communication. Mass media models and cultivates stereotypes, which institutional and societal factors then shape. The resulting stereotype segment is expressed in media and rejoins the pool of stereotypes available in the larger culture. We rely partly on concepts from earlier chapters, notably the relationship between economic development and culture in the discussion of youth culture (see Chapter 2), but also introduce complementary perspectives including social learning theory and cultivation theory.

In Chapter 6, "An Ecology of Ageism: Health Care from the Individual Out," we tackle the issue of ageism in health care. We provide a fictitious example of hospital interactions between an elderly patient, his daughter, a nurse, and a doctor, to illustrate the many ways in which ageism can permeate seemingly simple face-to-face interactions. Using Bronfenbrenner's ecological model of human development as a framework, we provide examples of how ageism operates at all different levels of an individual's environment. We conclude by reflecting on whether and how unageist health care really can be, drawing attention to the difficulty of arriving at a simple answer. We touch upon the influence of historical factors (as in Chapter 3), particularly in the discussion of the medicalization of aging.

In Chapter 7, "Peripheral Ageism in Employment: From Explanation to Action," we tackle the question of why both younger and older workers are disadvantaged in different ways. We use the term peripheral ageism to describe a pattern of prejudice and discrimination in which the middle-aged are the advantaged group, arguing that the explanation of peripheral ageism that we adopt has implications for the actions we believe we should take to stem ageism in the workplace. We propose a number of explanations of peripheral ageism: the overlapping prejudices explanation, the cognitive processes explanation (based on material about theories of ageism from Chapter 1), the incomplete authority shift explanation (based on material about economic development and culture from Chapter 2), the response to deviance explanation (based on material about frame analysis from Chapter 3), and the intersectionality explanation (based on material from Chapter 4).

In Chapter 8, "Three Ways to Use an Ideology: A Political Economy of Ageism," we return to the question of age-restricted communities, making the argument that we readily accept their existence in large part through the influence of ideologies. Ideologies, a concept similar to frames (introduced in Chapter 3), refers to a cultural reservoir of ideas that we use to interpret the reality around us. Using insights from the political economy of aging, we detail three uses for ideology: as a source of cultural images, as a way to appeal to the economic system, and as a way to create systems of rational problem solving. Each of these chapters refers to a specific context, but draws on material from Part I for guidance.

5 Mass Media and the Segmentation of Ageism
A Look at Stereotypes on Facebook

In 2011 and 2012, a group of researchers identified 84 non-commercial, public Facebook groups describing adults aged 60 or older. The researchers, Levy, Chung, Bedford, and Navrazhina (2013), used broad criteria to identify the groups, searching for the terms "old," "elderly," "aged" and all their synonyms based on a thesaurus. When they analyzed the groups they found, they discovered that all the group creators were younger than age 60, with an average age between 20 and 29 years, and that almost all the descriptions of the elderly were negative. The majority of the descriptions were not only unflattering, but what the authors termed "excoriating." Aligning with the greedy geezer stereotype of the elderly as taking more than their fair share of resources (Fairlie, 1988), these descriptions presented extremely negative views of the elderly, such as:

> Old people do not contribute to modern society at all. Their [sic] single and only meaning is to nag and to [expletive deleted] moan. Therefore, any OAP [Old Age Pensioner] that pass [sic] the age of 69 should immediately face a fire [sic] squad.
> (Facebook group description, cited in Levy et al., 2013, p. 173)

In line with these descriptions, the creators of the groups often recommended banning the elderly from activities such as driving (37 percent) and shopping (23 percent). A smaller percentage of the groups (26 percent) featured descriptions of the elderly that were infantilizing, aligning with the compassionate ageism stereotype of the elderly as frail and poor but deserving of help (Binstock, 1983). For instance, one group description compared the elderly to "a smaller, younger child… who cannot stand up for themselves [sic]" (cited in Levy et al., 2013, p. 174). In this chapter, we argue that this extremely negative ageism, although derived from general cultural stereotypes, flourishes due both to general societal factors and institutional factors specific to Facebook.

Unlike the narrowly defined stereotypes in the Facebook group descriptions, Western **culture**, the knowledge and characteristics of the society as a whole,

68 *Ageism in Context*

includes a wide variety of negative and positive stereotypes. But the ways in which the **mass media** (the means of communication including television, film, literature, and electronics) filter, shape, and convey these stereotypes depend on both institutional and societal factors. Hence, similar to **market segmentation**, which seeks to divide consumers based on their characteristics and the products they would be most likely to buy (Smith, 1956), mass media encourages what we term **stereotype segmentation**, the division of more general cultural stereotypes into a number of specific stereotype segments. For instance, one stereotype segment is the positive ageism of magazines that promote healthy and happy aging. Another stereotype segment is the negative ageism of youth cultures such as those surrounding music and social networking sites.

In this chapter, we trace the origins of the negative **ageism segment** in Facebook group descriptions. As shown in Figure 6.1, we propose that media inculcates general stereotypes, which institutional and societal factors then filter and shape into specific stereotype segments. Societal factors refer to general trends that can affect each stereotype segment differently. Institutional factors refer to the norms specific to a given medium. Of note, the same general stereotypes can lead to different stereotype segments. We argue that the resulting stereotype segments then enter the larger cultural pool, influencing the developing of other stereotype segments. To make this argument, we discuss other ageism segments, including those evident in children's television and films, children's classic literature, men's and women's magazines, music, and social media, as they relate to the ageism segment in Facebook group descriptions.

Modeling and Cultivation: The Vulnerable Minds of Children

Theories originating in psychology and **media studies** (the academic study of mass media) can provide particular insight into the importance of media in modeling and cultivating ageism. In this section, using social learning theory and cultivation theory, we argue that the original sources of the

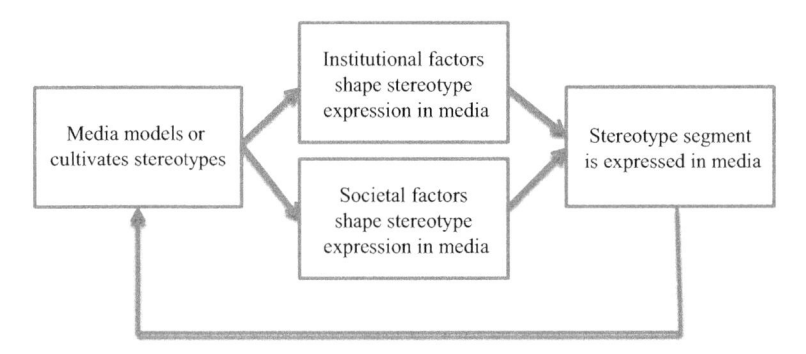

Figure 5.1 A model of stereotype segmentation

Facebook group descriptions are pervasive stereotypes that we learn beginning in childhood.

Social Learning Theory: From Aggression to Prejudice

One of the primary ways that media inculcates behaviors and attitudes is by providing **models**, individuals to observe and imitate. Psychologist Albert Bandura's (1978) social learning theory highlights the ways in which humans learn behavior through exposure to models, including: direct interactions, such as family and co-workers; community models, such as town and neighborhood dynamics; and media sources, such as television and the internet. When people, particularly children, observe media that includes particular beliefs and behaviors, they learn and emulate those behaviors.

Perhaps the most famous of Bandura's studies on modeling dealt with aggression among children. Bandura and his colleagues (Bandura, Ross, & Ross, 1961, 1963) performed the "Bobo doll" experiments with children approximately aged 3 to 6. In one experiment, after taking the child and an adult model into a room, the experimenter instructed the child to make potato prints or play with stickers. Meanwhile, the adult assembled tinker toys next to a 5 foot tall inflatable "Bobo" doll. For half of the children, the adult soon turned his or her attention to the Bobo doll, modeling physically and verbally aggressive behavior. For instance, he or she would hit the Bobo doll with a mallet while saying "Pow!" and then punch it repeatedly saying "Sock him in the nose." For the other half of the children, the adult continued to assemble the tinker toys, ignoring the Bobo doll. When the experimenters later observed the children in a room with toys and a 3 foot tall Bobo doll, they found that children who observed aggressive models behaved more aggressively than those who observed non-aggressive models. Many children who saw an aggressive model imitated him or her directly, acting and speaking in similar ways toward the Bobo doll (Bandura et al., 1963). The experiment provided scientific evidence of the startling impressionality of a child's mind.

The original Bobo doll experiment highlighted the importance of in-person models such as parents, teachers, and friends. But what about media sources, such as television? In a second experiment, Bandura and his colleagues (1963) exposed some of the children to the aggressive examples through films, either realistic or "cartoon" (in which the model dressed as a cartoon-style cat), rather than in person. They found that children who viewed aggressive models on film behaved just as aggressively as those who viewed aggressive models in person. Further, in both experiments, the children expanded on the modeled behavior, sometimes striking things aside from the Bobo doll with the mallet or lying on top of the doll but not hitting him. The Bobo doll experiments demonstrated that children could learn and expand on aggressive behavior from television.

To date, the most prominent vein of research using social learning theory remains the effect of media aggression on the behavior of boys and, to a lesser extent, girls (Snethen & Van Puymbroeck, 2008). However, a small body of research has used social learning theory as a framework for understanding discrimination. For example, Barclay (1982) uses Bandura's concept of expectations as a method for understanding discrimination. **Efficacy expectations** refer to the belief that a person can execute a behavior, while **outcome expectations** refer to the belief that a behavior leads to an outcome. These expectations are learned in part through modeling, which Barclay refers to as "vicarious experience." In the case of efficacy expectations, imagine a woman working as a firefighter. To the extent that she can execute the behaviors involved in the job (e.g., lifting the heavy firehose), she serves as a model that raises the efficacy expectations of others with regards to women. People observing her learn to expect that women can be competent firefighters. In the case of outcome expectations, imagine a woman striving to move into upper management at a large firm. She can perform the work tasks required to receive such a promotion, but she is not promoted. Her example lowers the outcome expectations for women; even if they do the job (high efficacy expectations), they will not receive the promotion (low outcome expectations). Barclay (1982) argues that social learning theory provides a lens for understanding prejudice and discrimination as learned behaviors. We might, for instance, learn low efficacy expectations of older adults from simplified media models of doddering grandparents.

Cultivation Theory: The Special Place of Television

While social learning theory is a **micro-level** theory dealing primarily with individuals and small groups, **cultivation theory** is its **macro-level** cousin, dealing with large groups or society as a whole. Communication scholar George Gerbner, in the development of cultivation theory, explains how macro-level trends in media cultivate assumptions about the world over a long time span (Potter, 2014). The more time we spend living in the symbolic worlds of mass media, the more we believe that the real world is like the symbolic world.

Gerbner and his team's original empirical efforts focused on mainstream television (Potter, 2014). In one 1980 article, they estimated that 55 percent of major characters suffered violence and 46 percent committed violence in dramatic television, rates far higher than in the real world. These unrealistic depictions of violence cultivated people's expectations of violence in their own lives. When they asked people in surveys, "What are your chances of being involved in some kind of violence during any given week" (Gerbner, Gross, Signorielli, & Morgan, 1980, p. 712), those who watched four or more hours of television per day were more likely to believe that they would be involved in violence than were those who watched two or fewer hours per day. The more time they spent watching violent television programming, the more they believed that violence was normal and even inevitable.

Violence and aggression remain persistent topics in cultivation theory today (Scharrer & Blackburn, 2018; Jamieson & Romer, 2014), but other topics include the relationship between television and such varied outcomes as love styles (Hetsroni, 2012), beliefs about cancer prevention (Lee & Niederdeppe, 2011), and materialism (Shrum, Lee, Burroughs, & Rindfleisch, 2011). To date, though, researchers have paid comparatively little attention to how mass media cultivates prejudice and discrimination in general and ageism in particular, despite the fact that Gerbner (2000) identifies the underrepresentation of older adults as a key way in which the symbolic reality of television differs from the real world.

The Modeling and Cultivation of Ageism

In line with social learning theory and cultivation theory, we argue that the limited numbers of older adults in children's media, combined with the simplistic depictions of those older adults, can lead to deeply ingrained ageist beliefs over time. Research on children's television programs (Robinson & Anderson, 2006) and movies (Zurcher & Robinson, 2018) indicates that, compared to the real-world population, older adults are noticeably underrepresented. Zurcher and Robinson (2018) analyze 42 Disney films released from 2004 to 2016 for the number of older characters, their physical features, and their mental and personality characteristics. They find that the average Disney film features 3.15 older characters, far less than a child would encounter in the real world. Arguably, the more time children spend watching movies in which there are few if any older adults, the more they believe that the marginalization of older adults and their disappearance from positions of responsibility is a part of normal aging.

Further, television and films often rely on stereotypes to convey stories quickly, sometimes within the space of half an hour or less. For instance, a television show might use the image of an old witch (i.e., hooked nose, high-pitched voice) to convey that an older character is "wicked." Because children can have difficulty differentiating between fantasy and reality, they may interpret these characters as accurate depictions of older adults rather than as convenient tropes (Robinson & Anderson, 2006). As in television, children's films often use archetypes or stereotypes of older adults as a way to convey the story. Zurcher and Robinson (2018) find that most older characters in Disney films correspond to archetypical roles, ranging from negative (e.g., shrew/curmudgeon) to positive (e.g., perfect grandparent). The use of these archetypes in film and television, combined with the underrepresentation of older adults, may cultivate ageism over time.

The Facebook Ageism Segment

We might be tempted to argue that the underrepresentation of older adults in children's media and film leads directly to the excoriating and infantilizing descriptions in the Facebook groups discussed at the beginning of this chapter. The exposure to ageist media probably plays a significant role but cannot be the whole story because the depictions of older adults in children's television and movies are often positive. For instance, in Zurcher and Robinson's (2018) study, 27 percent of older Disney characters fell into the perfect grandparent archetype and 24 percent fell into the sage archetype.

We argue that media provide a pool of stereotypes, including both positive and negative stereotypes. Hence, rather than exhibiting a simple relationship between television stereotypes and later beliefs, exposure to these stereotypes sets the stage for ageism by providing a pool of possible stereotypes. Both institutional and societal factors specific to each medium (e.g., television, internet) then filter and transform the stereotypes in unique ways, determining which stereotypes become expressed.

The Role of Societal Factors: The Life Spans of Youth Cultures

What factors filter and transform the pool of stereotypes that we absorb from the media? One source of filters is societal factors, such as general economic and cultural shifts, that can have different effects for different parts of the population. For instance, the trend toward extended periods of youth encourages the development of **youth cultures**, norms, activities, interests, and practices of youth, which may foster stereotype fragments distinct from the prevailing culture among young adults. Below, we argue that the ageism evident in Facebook group descriptions, whose group creators are predominately young adults, originates partly in youth culture.

Youth: The Invention of a Life Stage

Childhood and youth, as we understand them today, are relatively new social constructions. During the Middle Ages, children were fairly independent as early as age 7. A person's late teenage years through 20s, the ages that we now identify as their youth, were instead solidly located in the middle of adulthood. A number of related economic and social changes made youth an identifiable stage of life for most people living in industrialized countries, including: rising educational participation, particularly higher rates of college attendance; delayed labor market transitions, with many young adults working only part time until their early 20s; and extended periods of dependency, in which many people were fully or partly supported by their parents well into their 20s (Laughey,

2006). Youth as a life stage was a product partly of economic development.

Because growing numbers of adolescents were concentrated in schools and had substantial amounts of leisure time, they developed a culture that centered on leisure interests such as music genre rather than on employment or other "adult" concerns (Janssen, Deschesne, & Van Knippenberg, 1999). The resulting youth culture featured an underlying resistance to adult norms and responsibilities. In an influential 1972 article, sociologist Talcott Parsons argued that youth culture is fundamentally irresponsible, focused on "having a good time" and on rejecting adult interests, expectations, and discipline. Further, as Janssen et al. (1999) detail, people's allegiance to youth culture is related to a fear of mortality. The more immediate people's fears of mortality, the more they cling to youth as a concept and a lifestyle. Hence, the primary shared element of youth cultures is their rejection of the responsibilities and norms of middle adulthood, but a secondary element is an avoidance of the eventual mortality of later adulthood.

Aside for the underlying resistance to adulthood, youth cultures are diverse. A number of separate **youth subcultures**, or cultural groupings within the larger youth culture, tend to coexist, each with their own representative presentation styles. For instance, in the Netherlands, as many as ten different youth cultures existed within the larger youth culture of the 1980s. These included: disco, flower power, hard rock, *kak* (posh), new wave, *normalo* (average), punk, Rastafari, rock, and skinhead (Janssen et al., 1999). As the original fans of each type of music aged, youth cultures shifted over time, as cultures such as rock and goth in the United States evidence.

The Examples of Rock and Goth: The Afterlife of Youth Cultures

Some people continue to participate in youth cultures through middle and later adulthood. Studies of rock (Bennett, 2018), goth (Hodkinson, 2012), and punk (Bennett, 2006) cultures indicate that people who remain involved in previously youth cultures individualize their participation over time. For instance, they might select fewer night-time events to attend or tone down their clothing choices to avoid adversely affecting their work advancement (Hodkinson, 2012). The process is gradual, and affects both the individual's choices and the general atmosphere of the culture itself.

Rock culture provides an example of this process. The Baby Boom and post-World War II affluence created a generation of teenagers with substantial amounts of disposable income, much of which they spent on music-related technologies such as vinyl 45' records. While earlier genres, such as jazz, originally appealed to people of all ages, rock music targeted youth markets from its inception. By the 1960s, music artists such as the Beatles, the Rolling Stones, Bob Dylan, and Jimi Hendrix brought a new dimension to rock culture, using it as a means to champion sociopolitical change (Bennett, 2018). Part of rock culture was a rejection of the status quo and a distrust of adults in middle and later life. As activist Jack Weinberg famously told a reporter, "Don't trust anyone over 30" (Daily Planet Staff, 2000). Over time, the fans of rock music aged, resulting in a gradual redefinition of rock culture without the youth focus.

Goth culture provides a more recent example. It arose in the early 1980s among predominantly white and middle-class teenagers and was, until the later 1990s, "dominated by youth in their teens and early twenties and characterised by familiar forms of youthful hedonism and transgression" (Hodkinson, 2012, p. 1076). Goth culture also rejected the prevailing adult culture by challenging gender boundaries through both androgynous personal appearance and acceptance of gender fluidity. By the early 2010s, the average age of goths had increased and increasing numbers of goths were becoming parents. The "goth baby boom" resulted not only in affectionate terms such as "baby bats," but also in the normalization of parenthood and children in goth culture (Hodkinson, 2012). Similar to rock culture, goth culture retained its focus on characteristic music and clothing, but gradually shifted away from its ageist subtext.

Digital Youth Cultures

A small but growing body of literature discusses "digital" (Rafalow, 2018) or "mobile" (Vanden Abeele, 2016) youth cultures, which surround both particular platforms (e.g., Facebook, Instagram) and the pervasive use of the internet as a whole. Social media use is highest among younger adults. Eighty-eight percent of those aged 18 to 29 use some form of social media, compared to only 37 percent of those aged 65 and older (see Figure 5.2). Although Facebook has the oldest user demographic of popular social media sites, only 41 percent of Americans aged 65 and older use it (Smith & Anderson, 2018). We argue here that the age demographic of Facebook promotes what we term a **partial youth culture**, a culture with a relatively young age demographic, but one that includes a substantial number of middle-aged and older adults. We posit that the extreme nature of the excoriating and infantilizing descriptions, together with the almost complete absence of positive stereotypes of the elderly, stems in part from the "youthful" skew of Facebook's demographic. While the creation of youth as a life stage is a general societal trend, it affects the expression of ageism differently depending on the medium. Like musical styles, digital media may have a tendency to give rise to youth cultures due to their appeal to younger people.

The Role of Institutional Factors: The Suppression of Gendered Ageism

Just as general societal trends can influence the development of ageism segments, institutional factors also play a role. To illustrate the role of institutional factors in filtering and shaping stereotypes, consider a strange omission

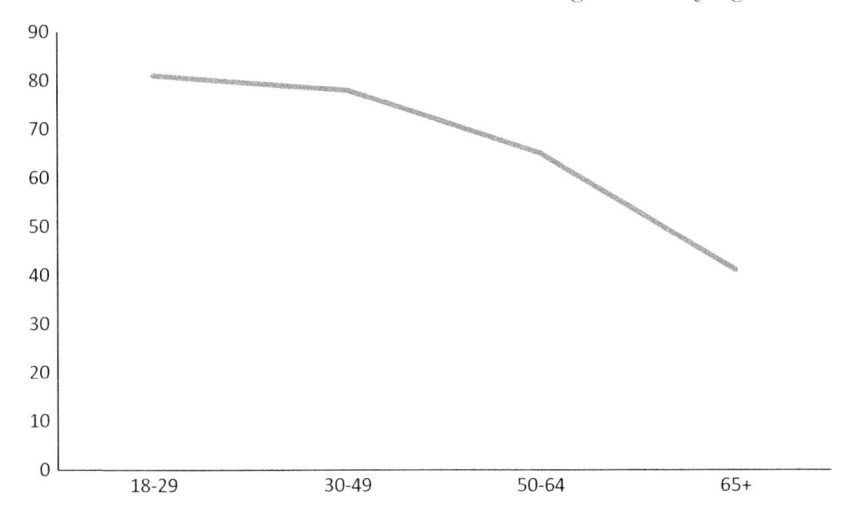

Figure 5.2 Percentage of U.S. adults who say that they use Facebook, by age
Source: Smith & Anderson, 2018

in the Facebook group descriptions. As we discussed in Chapter 4, intersectionality—the interconnections between experiences and perceptions of social categories including race and ethnicity, age, sexual orientation, and gender—permeates stereotypes and discrimination. In particular, ageism tends to be gendered, with distinctly different stereotypes for men and women. But the Facebook descriptions, as Levy et al. (2013) report them, are not gendered. They do not focus on frail old women or querulous old men, but rather on the elderly in general. Below, we detail how gendered ageism dominates both children's and adults' media, then discuss the role of institutional factors in suppressing these gendered stereotypes and instead promoting the ungendered descriptions on Facebook.

Witches, Godmothers, and Hags: Gendered Ageism in Children's Literature

Classic children's literature provides some of the clearest examples of gendered ageism, in which sexism and ageism converge. Regarding sexism, children's stories often minimize or eliminate the role of the mother. The children in the stories are sometimes orphans, as in Johanna Spyri's *Heidi* and Ludwig Bemelman's *Madeline*. When a parent survives, as in the Nancy Drew series, it is typically the father. If the mother survives, her role in the story is minimal. For instance, Dr. Seuss' *The Cat in the Hat* reduces the mother to a pair of shoes. Evil stepmothers, as in *Snow White* and *Hansel and Gretel*, replace the good mother (Henneberg, 2010). These stories feature a young or middle-aged adult female character as "evil" rather than as "good."

Grandmothers and grandmother-like characters appear regularly, and the stereotypes of older women are distinct from the stereotypes of younger and middle-aged women. As professor of English Sylvia Henneberg (2010) argues in her analysis of children's literature, "women… fare badly, but old women do even worse" (p. 125). She states that literary grandmothers fall into three main types: wicked old witches (as in *Hansel and Gretel*), selfless godmothers (as in *Cinderella*), and ineffectual hags (as in *Sleeping Beauty*). While the selfless godmothers present a counterpoint, the prevailing stereotypes of older women in children's classic literature are as evil or ineffectual. The "selfless" older woman is a less frequent figure.

Women's Magazines, Men's Magazines: Gendered Ageism in Adults' Media

Media targeted toward adults, such as magazines, has also included evidence of a deeply gendered ageism. **Content analysis** (i.e., systematic analysis of media) of magazines and advertisements reveals an under-representation of older adults of both genders. For instance, researchers Clarke, Bennett, and Liu (2014) analyze representations of later life in six North American magazines (*Esquire, GQ, Maxim, Men's Health, Men's Journal*, and *Zoomer*). They begin by analyzing images and texts of men over 65, but find that magazines do not even include enough of this age group to analyze. Even when they lower the age to 50, as shown in Figure 5.3, fewer than 30 percent of the images in each magazine except *Zoomer* portray older men. Similarly, in Twigg's (2018) content analysis and interviews of personnel at four United Kingdom women's magazines, she finds that two of the magazines (*Vogue* and *Woman & Home*) avoid using older models. This is notable in the case of *Woman & Home*, which has a readership of women concentrated in later middle age. Twigg cites strategies, such as showing clothing intended for older women without using an older model, that both target older women and exclude them.

In these magazines, the images of older adults are likely to be positive, but highly gendered. For instance, *Zoomer*, a Canadian lifestyle magazine targeting middle-aged and older adults, features "cover stars" such as actors and actresses (e.g., Helen Mirren, Christopher Plummer), musicians (e.g., Tony Bennett, Harry Belafonte), and writers (e.g., John Irving, Margaret Atwood), in their 40s and beyond. The magazine promotes the stars as examples of successful aging, often including the stars' age and a message stating "I'm one," "He's one," or "She's one" next (Marshall & Rahman, 2014). For men's magazines, as in Clarke et al.'s (2014) study, most images depict older men either as powerful and important members of society or as healthy and happy. Women's magazines, as in Twigg's (2018) study, are likely to depict older women as fashionable. "Decade" features, which show women how to dress at 20, 30, 40, and so on, explicitly include the idea of women remaining fashionable as they age. When the magazines include

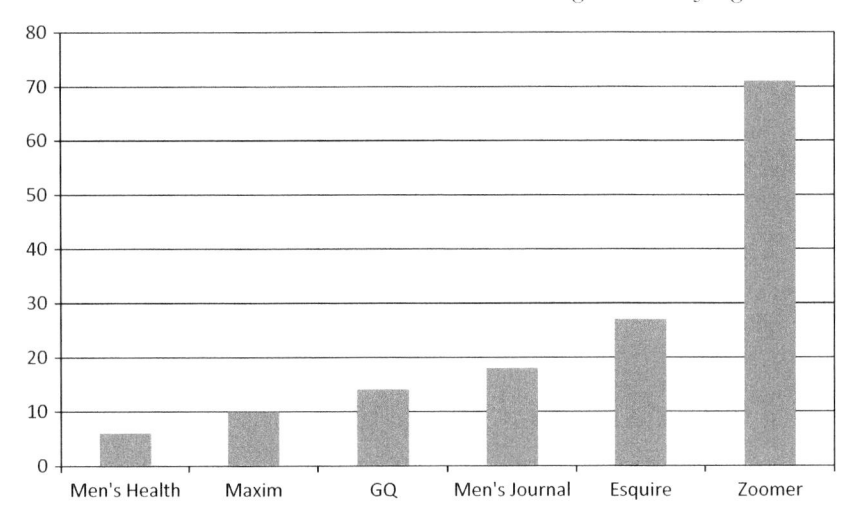

Figure 5.3 Percentage of images of men aged 50+ in six magazines
Source: Clarke, Bennett, & Liu, 2014

older women as models, they are often glamorous celebrities or women receiving fashion makeovers. The combination of an underrepresentation of older adults and a positive image of those who do appear is telling. The ageism is implicit not in the content, but in the relative lack of content of older adults.

The Ungendered Ageism of Facebook Group Descriptions

Gendered ageism is prevalent both in children's classic literature and adults' magazines, but the forms that ageism can take differ depending on the specific media. For instance, the ungendered nature of the ageism in Facebook group descriptions differs both from the children's literature stereotypes (i.e., older women as ineffectual or evil) and the adults' magazines stereotypes (i.e., older men as powerful or happy and older women as fashionable). We argue that Facebook provides an example of how institutional factors specific to a medium shape ageist segments. As Levy et al. (2013) note, Facebook's Community Standards forbids singling individuals out based on "sex, gender, sexual orientation, disability or disease" (Facebook's 2012 standards, cited in Levy et al., 2013, p. 173). The Community Standards offer no reference to age itself. Hence, the standards are likely to suppress the creation of groups targeting old women or old men, while allowing for the creation of groups targeting older people in general.

Times Are Changing: The Future of Segmented Ageism?

The example of Facebook group descriptions demonstrates how societal and institutional factors can filter and shape stereotypes. But, it is crucial to recognize that, once established, ageism segments become part of the cultural reservoir of stereotypes about the aged. For instance, the forms of media explored in this chapter each contribute to our ideas about older adults. Future ageisms depend partly on the ageism segments included in each medium, and how those ageisms interact and change over time.

We argue that ageism is likely to become more, rather than less, segmented over time. Media appeal to and fit certain niches of consumers, such as younger adults or women, due in part to targeted marketing efforts and in part to the nature of medium. And, to the extent that media become more varied and offer more choice, they also allow for the creation of more ageist segments. Technological and social changes that allow for the success of numerous social media sites, each of which appeals to different audiences such as women or younger adults (Smith & Anderson, 2018), may lead to further differentiation of segments. Similarly, because streaming services such as Netflix and Amazon Prime do not need to appeal to ratings or advertising as traditional television does, the trend is toward more individuated programming. Hence, series such as *Transparent* and *The Good Wife* include a wide variety of older characters than mainstream television generally does (Givskov & Petersen, 2018). The combination between more varied stereotypes about the elderly in television programs and social media and the ability of people to intentionally choose the media that meet their needs suggest that ageism is likely to become more, rather than less, segmented over time.

Conclusion

In this chapter, we made the argument that ageism in the mass media is segmented, and that these segments reflect not only general stereotypes, but also how societal and institutional factors shape those stereotypes over time. We discussed a wide range of media, including children's television and film, children's classic literature, men's and women's magazines, social media sites, and rock and goth music. Overall, we argue that the excoriating and infantilizing descriptions of the elderly on Facebook groups reflect a number of factors, including an existing pool of both negative and positive views of the elderly, societal factors such as the development of youth cultures, and institutional factors such as the community standards of the website.

Discussion Questions

1 Sociologist Barbara Marshall (2015) argues that **anti-ageist** messages in our media are ultimately about growing older without the supposed negative aspects of aging, such as physical and mental decline. Are anti-ageist stereotypes realistic for the elderly? Are anti-ageist stereotypes good for the elderly?

2 The Facebook group descriptions in Levy et al.'s (2013) study were captured in 2011 and 2012. Try searching Facebook groups or another social media sites for evidence of positive ageism. Do your findings differ from what Levy et al. (2013) reported? How do you think the stereotypes of the elderly evidence on social media will change over time?

6 An Ecology of Ageism
Health Care from the Individual Out

A nurse enters a hospital room where an 85-year-old patient has recently received a diagnosis of lung cancer. She asks, "How are we feeling? Is your daughter visiting today?" He replies, "I can't remember if she's visiting today… at my age, my memory isn't what it used to be." After the nurse leaves, the patient's daughter arrives, followed by a physician. The physician begins discussing treatment options with the man's daughter. Unfortunately, because the man has numerous physical limitations, he is ineligible for many experimental treatments. While aggressive treatments are available, he may not tolerate them well. Options for palliative care in their state are limited, but there is a palliative care unit at a nearby hospital that they can consider. The daughter says they need time to think about these options.

The example given above is fictitious, but it resonates with the experience of many people who have experienced health care for older adults, either for themselves or for a loved one. Everyone in the example is trying to provide good health care, but the way in which they do so reveals a number of ageist beliefs and assumptions. Below, using this fictitious example, we explore how ageism plays out using insights from the **ecological model of human development**, a context-focused theory from **developmental psychology** (the study of human change over the life span). As you read about the various types of ageism in health care, consider whether a truly non-ageist approach is both possible and desirable.

The Ecological Model of Human Development: Putting Development in Context

In this chapter, we use the ecological model of human development, a context-focused theory from developmental psychology, to examine ageism in health care. Until the early 1970s, most people working in the field of developmental psychology relied on laboratory experiments for the bulk of their data. These experiments were typically short term and focused on the reaction of children to specific stimuli such as puzzles. While the experimental approach aimed to be rigorous, it removed contextual factors, particularly patterns of behavior that developed over long periods of time.

Because of this, psychologist Urie Bronfenbrenner (1977) criticized the developmental psychology of the time as "the science of the strange behavior of children in strange situations with strange adults for the briefest possible periods of time" (p. 513). He argued that a real perspective on human development should take the opposite approach, focusing on long-term patterns and social context. In his *Ecology of Human Development* (1979) and subsequent writing, he developed an ecological model which attempted to locate the individual's development at the center of a number of subsystems such as family and school.

Bronfenbrenner (2000) considered **proximal processes**, the interactions between the individual and those in their immediate environment, to be the most immediate causes of human development. Proximal processes that endured over long time spans, such as the relationship between the daughter and the patient in the example, tended to become particularly complex. Further, as shown in Figure 6.1, proximal processes depended on the ecological environment, the set of nested subsystems, including microsystems, mesosystems, exosystems, macrosystems, and chronosystems, that surrounded the individual. The **microsystem** referred to activities, roles, and relationships that occurred in face-to-face settings such as the family, workplace, or hospital. **Mesosystems** were the linkages between two or more settings, such family and school, in which the developing person participated. **Exosystems** were the linkages between two or more settings,

Individual
- includes both biological and social attributes
- e.g., internalized beliefs about age and health

Microsystem
- systems of face-to-face relationships, such as family and school
- e.g., underdiagnosis of pain and depression, elderspeak

Mesosystem
- connections between two or more microsystems within which the individual is directly located
- e.g., triadic communications between physicians, patients, and companions

Exosystem
- connections between one microsystem within which the individual is directly located, and one "outside" microsystem
- e.g., relationships between hospital and related health-care systems

Macrosystem
- larger cultural patterns
- cultural beliefs about age and health care

Chronosystem
- changes over time
- e.g., medicalization of aging

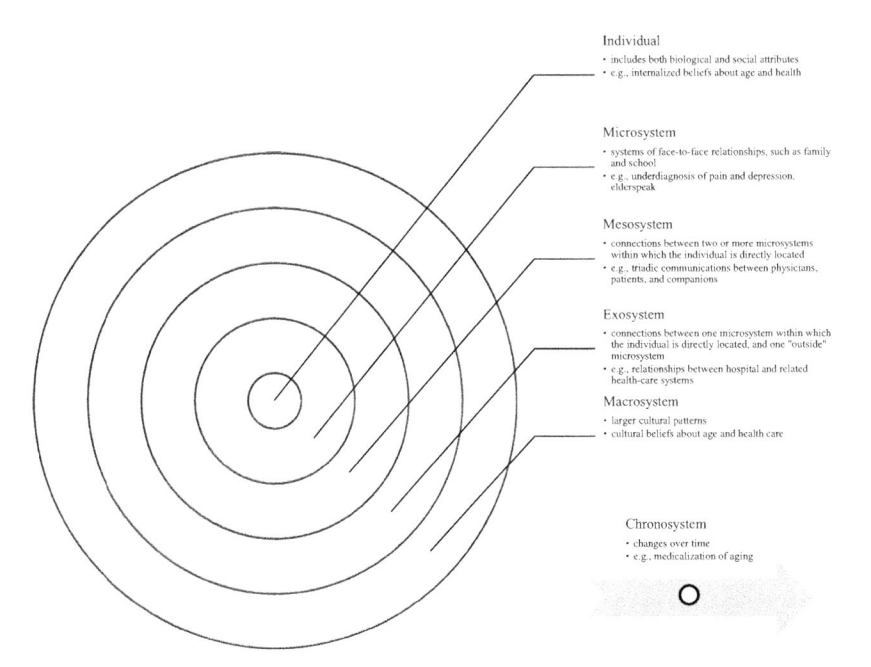

Figure 6.1 Ecological model of development

one of which the developing individual participated in and one of which the individual was outside. **Macrosystems** referred to the overarching patterns of systems that characterized a culture. **Chronosystems** extended the other systems into the "third dimension" of time, including both individual time such as chronological age and historical time such as changes in the typical family structure.

Extending the Ecological Model to the Older Adult in Health Care

While Bronfenbrenner's work deals mostly with childhood development, in this chapter we extend his model to older adults, beginning at the individual level and moving outward through macrosystems and chronosystems. We argue that ageism permeates the context surrounding older adults, and that it can affect their development, particularly their trajectories of mental health, cognitive status, and physical health, much as prejudice and discrimination can affect the long-term development of children. At the individual level, we discuss self-stereotyping and stereotype threat as ways in which individual-level beliefs about age and aging come into play in medical settings. We then highlight underdiagnosis of pain and depression among older adults and elderspeak as manifestations of ageism in the microsystem of the hospital. We discuss the connection between the family and hospital as an aspect of the mesosystem and between the hospital and other health-care-related systems as aspects of the exosystem. To evaluate the impact of cultural beliefs in the macrosystem, we examine two approaches to the allocation of medical care. Finally, to illustrate the importance of the chronosystem, we focus on the medicalization of aging as an aspect of historical time. Throughout, we illustrate how the proximal processes in the fictitious story above depend on how beliefs about age and ageing play out at each of these levels.

The Individual: Cognition, Emotion, and the Older Adult Stereotype

The effects of proximal processes at any given point in time depend partly on the individual's characteristics, both those that originate in "nature," such as genetic predispositions, and those attributable to "nurture," such as attitudes inculcated over time. Bronfenbrenner (1994) placed special importance on biological factors, prompting him to relabel his model the "bio"ecological model of human development in his later work. In this section, we instead focus on stereotypes that people internalize over a lifetime as examples of how ageism operates at the individual level. Many widely known stereotypes, particularly those based on ascribed characteristics such as race, gender, and age, precede the individual. People are aware of a wide range of negative stereotypes of older adults, such as being "stuck in their ways" and being "frail," before they become older adults themselves. For instance, the older man says his memory is poor due to his age. But, given that these stereotypes are often negative and can be untrue of the individual, how is it possible that people adopt the stereotypes when the target is themselves? Existing research suggests that there are both cognitive and emotional aspects to this phenomenon.

Cognition: Self-Stereotyping

Self-stereotyping refers to the cognitive phenomenon of individuals ascribing characteristics to themselves based on existing in-group stereotypes. Previous research has shown that lower-status groups are more likely to engage in self-stereotyping than are higher-status groups. Latrofa, Vaes, and Cadinu (2012) suggest that members of lower-status groups attempt to increase the status of their vulnerable in-group by affiliating with that group. Members of higher-status groups, such as men, are likely to individuate instead, rejecting the group stereotype in favor of their individual identity. For example, Cadinu and Galdi (2012) report data in which men and women match words related to the self (e.g., *I, me*) and others (e.g., *theirs, yours*) to words related to masculine (e.g., *independent, powerful*) and feminine (e.g., *affectionate, sensitive*) stereotypes. As members of the lower-status group, women are more likely to automatically associate themselves with the female stereotype (Cadinu & Galdi, 2012; Latrofa et al., 2012). From this perspective, self-stereotyping is an extension of the observations of social identity theory. This approach works as a cognitive strategy used to bolster self-esteem by embracing group membership.

We argue that the elderly, like women, may be more likely to stereotype themselves due to the relatively low status of the elderly compared to younger and middle-aged adults. For instance, research using word recall tests has shown that people often stereotype themselves as having poor memories as they age (O'Brien & Hummert, 2006). Further, the elderly differ from most demographic groups in that people age into the in-group. Hence, they may have already adopted the stereotype of the elderly, but then accept those stereotypes as true of themselves when they reach "that age."

Emotion: Stereotype Threat

Another reason that people might appear to accept stereotypes directed toward themselves is emotional. Members of stereotyped groups know that they risk confirming stereotypes through their behavior. For instance, a woman who becomes emotional during a work meeting risks activating a stereotype ("Women are overly emotional"), while co-workers are more likely to excuse a man for the same behavior ("He is just having a bad day"). Psychologists Steele and Aronson (1995) have termed this phenomenon **stereotype threat**, the threat of confirming or being judged according to a stereotype. This threat can activate emotional responses such as anxiety and fear, which can in turn cause the person to inadvertently confirm the stereotype through their behavior.

Consider, for example, the results of Steele and Aronson's (1995) study of black and white college students. The students were presented with a difficult test of verbal ability. Some participants believed that the test was evaluative, intended to examine "personal factors involved in performance on problems requiring reading and verbal reasoning abilities" (Steele & Aronson, 1995, p. 799) and other participants believed that the test was non-evaluative, intended to help build understanding of the "psychological factors involved in solving verbal problems" (Steele & Aronson, 1995, p. 799). Black students, for whom a test of personal intellectual ability posed a threat of confirming a racial stereotype of lower academic ability, performed more poorly when they believed that the test was an evaluation of their personal abilities.

The elderly can respond to a similar type of stereotype threat: measurement of their memory or intellectual capacity (Armstrong, Gallant, Li, Patel, & Wong, 2017). Older adults who believe that they are taking part in a memory test risk confirming the stereotype of poor memories and can underperform due to anxiety (Horton, Baker, Pearce, & Deakin, 2010). For instance, they perform more poorly on word-recall tests when their age is mentioned as a potential factor (O'Brien & Hummert, 2006). The combination of cognitive and emotional factors at the individual level means that the elderly often stereotype themselves, as the patient in the example does when he describes his memory as poor.

The Microsystem: What We Say and How We Say It

Many of the most obvious examples of ageism take place in microsystems, the relationships, roles, and activities that occur in face-to-face interactions. For a child, the most important microsystems might include the family and the school. For the older adult in the example, the most important microsystems might include the family and the hospital. In this section, we examine how "what we say" (the treatments that the medical professionals offer) and "how we say it" (the use of elderspeak) demonstrates the existence of ageism in the microsystem of the hospital.

What We Say: Underdiagnosis and Treatment of Pain and Depression

Pain is one of the most commonly undiagnosed and undertreated conditions among older adults (Ouchida & Lachs, 2015). Given that the estimated prevalence of pain is between 25 and 88 percent of elderly adults (Bonnewyn et al., 2009), it is not surprising that many primary care clinicians consider pain an "expected" or normal part of aging (Davis, Bond, Howard, & Sarkisian, 2011). But this can gloss over the amount of pain that is treatable. For instance, as shown in Figure 6.2, the largest age-related increases in pain are attributable to low back pain. Some other types of pain actually decrease with age (U.S. Department of Health and Human Services, 2017). The stereotype of pain as part of normal aging may lead to underdiagnosis of treatable pain.

Similarly, estimates suggest that between 1 and 5 percent of older people have major depression, and between 3 and 26 percent have depressive symptoms (Bonnewyn et al., 2009). However, undertreatment of depression is common, particularly for certain populations of the elderly, including the oldest old, the chronically ill, those with a cognitive impairment, and women. One study followed elderly adults over the course of nine years. Almost one third of those with persistent depression received no depression treatment at all (Barry, Abou, Simen, & Gill, 2012). To the extent that "feeling down" is stereotyped as a normal part of old age, depression is likely to go untreated.

How We Say It: Elderspeak

While underdiagnosis and undertreatment due to ageist stereotypes are potentially harmful to elderly patients, ageism in microsystems is evident not only in "what we say" but also in "how we say it." For example, in the anecdote above, the nurse asks, "How are we feeling?" This is an example of **elderspeak**, the patronizing talk directed toward the elderly. Elderspeak is widespread and ironically stems from the tendency of humans to try to reduce social distance by accommodating others in their communication style. As we discussed briefly in the Introduction, elderspeak starts from

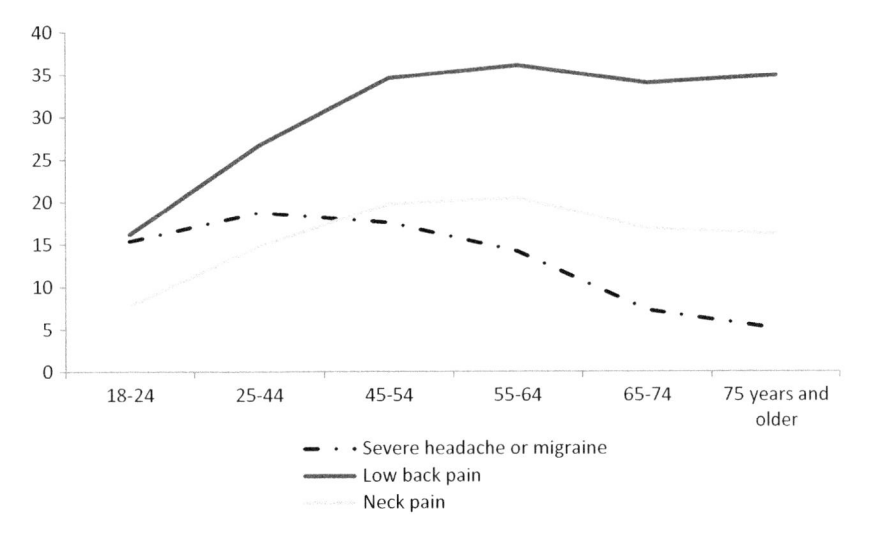

Figure 6.2 Prevalence of three types of pain, by age
Source: U.S. Department of Health and Human Services, 2017

good intentions and may, in part, be a response to the lower health of many older adults. But in many cases, it goes too far.

Psychologist Howard Giles and his colleagues developed **communication accommodation theory** in part to understand phenomena such as elderspeak. His theory provided a framework for understanding how individuals used verbal and non-verbal communication to reduce, maintain, or accentuate the social distance between themselves and their audience. People belonged to multiple in-groups, and each in-group had distinctive verbal and non-verbal communication styles. For instance, people from different regions of the United States spoke in dialects and used regional colloquialisms, and people from different generations used specific slang terms and idioms. The greater the differences in communication styles between an individual and their audience, the more that communication maintained or increased social distance rather than reducing it. While **divergence**, which accentuated the verbal and non-verbal differences between the speaker and their audience, and **maintenance**, which adhered to the original communication style regardless of the audience, occurred in a wide variety of contexts, perhaps the most common type of communicative accommodation was **convergence**. In convergence, individuals closed the social distance with their audiences by accommodating the audience's communication style, often downplaying differences (Giles & Ogay, 2006). Communication accommodation can help to bring people from different social backgrounds closer together.

If accommodation downplays social distance, as Giles and his colleagues show, why is elderspeak offensive to so many people? The answer is that accommodation is not always successful. Imagine that a teenager, when communicating with her grandparents, avoids slang. She implicitly understands that the use of these terms will increase social distance by emphasizing the existence of an in-group to which the older adult does not belong. To avoid this, she converges toward the grandparents' style of communication, successfully reducing social distance. Now imagine that the grandparent instead tries to accommodate the teenager's communication style by using terms that they believe the teenager normally uses (e.g., terms from online communication, such as "OMG"). If the teenager views these accommodations as patronizing or artificial, the grandparent might inadvertently increase social distance rather than decrease it. **Overaccommodation**, in which the person makes too many or inappropriate accommodations in communication, occurs in a wide variety of settings, but elderspeak is among the most familiar.

Elderspeak is a form of overaccommodation in which people unsuccessfully try to close the gap between themselves and the elderly (Giles & Ogay, 2006). Common in medical settings (Williams, Perkhounkova, Herman, & Bossen, 2017), it has both verbal and non-verbal elements, many of which reflect the stereotype of the elderly as incompetent. According to one study, over 80 percent of interactions in transcripts between nursing home residents and staff include some form of elderspeak. Figure 6.3 shows results from this study. The most common type is collective pronoun substitutions

An Ecology of Ageism 87

Type	Yes	No
Any elderspeak	67	13
Collective pronoun substitution	55	25
Diminutives	42	38
Tag questions	39	41
Reflective forms	11	69

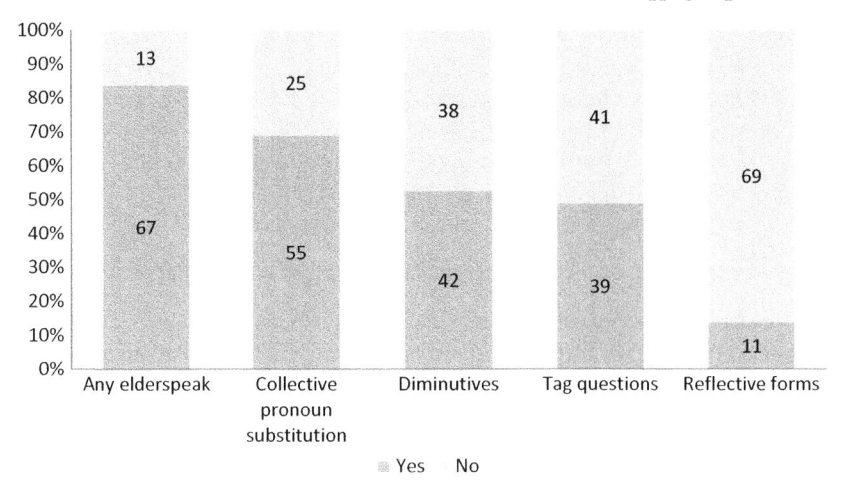

Figure 6.3 Types of elderspeak
Source: Based on a study of 80 nursing home transcripts, reported in Williams et al., 2017

including referring to residents as "we" rather than "you." Other common features of elderspeak include diminutives, inappropriately used language or terms of endearment such as "honey," and tag questions which restrict conversation by indicating desired responses (e.g., "You want eggs for breakfast, don't you?"). (Williams et al., 2017). Sentence structure and length are also elements of elderspeak. In one study, a group of physicians and medical students explain an endocrine therapy to 40-year-old and 70-year-old fictitious patients. The medical professionals use more repetitions and fewer words per utterance when explaining the treatment to the fictitious 70 year old, as compared to the 40 year old (Shroyen et al., 2017). Medical staff often view this style of communication as somewhat appropriate among certain populations, including patients age 70 and older and cognitively impaired patients (Lombardi et al., 2014). But the statistics in Figure 6.3 suggest that it is common even in situations where we would see it as inappropriate.

However well intentioned, elderspeak in medical settings can have a number of related, negative effects. First, overaccommodation can appear patronizing, artificial, and alienating, reducing compliance and increase resistance to care due to the resentment that elderly patients feel toward medical professionals (Williams et al., 2017). Second, by emphasizing the incompetence and lower social status of the older adult, elderspeak can prime them with negative views of themselves, beginning a downward spiral of lower cognitive and physical performance (Williams et al., 2009). Elderspeak is associated with lower cognitive performance among some populations of older adults as they internalize negative views of themselves. And, as research on non-human primates has shown, when people find themselves in subordinate positions, cortisol helps to provide the energy to overcome short-term social threats. Since elderspeak places older adults in a socially subordinate position repeatedly, the frequent activation of cortisol places stress on their bodies (Hehman & Bugental, 2015). What we know about elderspeak is almost entirely negative, but it remains one of the most persistent forms of ageism in medical contexts.

Mesosystems and Exosystems: Ageism Where Systems Meet

Meso and exosystems refer to the interactions between two or more systems that affect an individual's development. Mesosystems concern the connections between systems in which the individual is directly involved, such as the connections between the family and hospital. Exosystems refer to the connections between one system in which the individual is directly involved and one system in which the individual is not directly involved. An aspect of the exosystem of importance to older adults is the relationship between the hospital and other systems which affect the availability and quality of care.

Triadic Interactions: Where Health Care and Family Meet

In the fictitious example at the beginning of this chapter, the patient's adult daughter is part of the interaction with the physician, an aspect of the mesosystem linking the family and the hospital. Triadic medical interactions, consisting of the patient, the medical professional, and a companion, are common (Wolff & Roter, 2011). In particular, spouses and adult children (Wolff, Boyd, Gitlin, Bruce, & Roter, 2011) are likely to accompany older adults who have lower education or mental and physical health limitations (Wolff & Roter, 2011). These interactions have the potential to be positive, involving caregivers more directly in medical care. However, there is currently little guidance about what role the companion or caregiver should play. Consequently, the elderly patient is sometimes marginalized during important parts of the interaction. Elderly patients speak fewer words and contribute to the dialogue less when a companion is present at their medical appointment (Laidsaar-Powell et al., 2013). Further, triadic conversations often break down into dyadic conversations from which the elderly are excluded. Karnieli-Miller, Werner, Neufeld-Kroszynski, and Eidelman (2012) analyze 25 triadic encounters in which memory clinic physicians disclose Alzheimer's diagnoses to elderly patients and their companions. The physicians often determine how much and when the companion and the patient are able to speak, moving to a dyadic conversation between themselves and the companion when they discuss treatment options. One patient in the study describes her frustration, saying "I asked her, 'Is there a pill I have to take? Do I have any problem?' She told me, 'I'll talk with your daughter… Elderly persons forget'" (p. 386). To the extent that the physician, companion, or elderly adult bring ageist stereotypes to the interaction, the elderly patient is at risk of being excluded from critical decision making about their treatment.

Geriatric Health Care: Connections to Clinical Trials

Exosystems refer to the linkages between two or more settings, only one of which the developing individual participates in. Due partly to negative attitudes toward older patients, there is a shortage of geriatricians, physicians focusing on older adults, both in teaching positions and in medical practices. Additionally, many clinical trials exclude older adults with multiple comorbidities and impairments. Given the extremely high rates of **comorbidity**, in which a person has more than one disease, among older adults, most adults above 70 or 80 years old are excluded from these trials (Ouchida & Lachs, 2015). In the case of the older patient in the fictitious example, this prevents him from being eligible for experimental treatments.

The Macrosystem: Age and Medical Allocation

In the fictitious example, the patient hears that palliative care options are relatively limited. One possible reason that palliative care options are not consistently available is the subtly ageist assumptions of the methods we use to evaluate the effectiveness of various treatments. These cultural assumptions are part of the macrosystem, the set of larger cultural patterns surrounding micro, meso, and exosystems. In this section, we describe two ways of allocating health care and highlight ways in which ageism may be present in both: the quality-adjusted life years measure prevalent in health economics and the fair innings argument familiar in medical ethics. We discuss how both of these methods of health allocation can de-emphasize certain treatments, such as palliative care.

Choosing between Medical Treatments: QALYs

Health economists often use a measure known as **aggregated quality-adjusted life years** (**QALYs**, from Zeckhauser and Shepard, 1976) to compare the cost-effectiveness of two or more treatments. They assign a QALY, or score ranging from 0 ("Death") to 1 ("Perfect health"), to each year of life that a treatment would grant, then sum those scores to evaluate the effect of the treatment. Based on these figures, they can then estimate which treatments are more cost-effective in terms of expected number and quality of years of remaining life. To see how this plays out, imagine that you have a hypothetical disease. Treatment A ($120,000) would certainly allow you to live the rest of your life at 50 percent of full health. It would provide 60 years of additional life at 50 percent of full health, or 30 QALYs at $4,000 per QALY. Treatment B (also $120,000) has only a 45 percent chance of success. If it fails, you will die shortly. If it is successful, you will return to full health. It would provide a 45 percent chance of 60 years of additional life at full health, or 27 QALYs at $5,000 per QALY. Ignoring how you might feel personally about choosing between a high risk of death (Treatment B) and a near certainty of lifetime disability (Treatment A), Treatment A is more cost-efficient.

The relationship of QALY maximization to ageism is subtle. Since the approach itself ignores the characteristics of the patients receiving care, it can appear explicitly anti-ageist (Harris, 1985). One QALY at age 10 is just as valuable as one QALY at age 90. But QUALY maximization involves an element of **utilitarian ageism** due to the lower life expectancies of older people. In an actual analysis of the cost-effectiveness of two medical treatments, the QALYs are summed over a large population of individuals. Because younger individuals have longer life expectancies, life-saving treatments can provide greater numbers of years of life for them. Saving a younger person "counts" for more than saving an older person (Tsuchiya, 2000). On an individual level, this places more weight on the younger person's life. On a population level, the QALY-maximization approach might steer us away from treatments that disproportionately target the elderly.

Choosing between Patients: Fair Innings

Given the difficulty that even anti-ageist approaches such as QALY maximization have being truly age-neutral, it is not surprising that some ways to make decisions about medical care instead take age into account. Particularly in cases of scarce resources, it appears to make sense to take age into account. Philosopher John Harris, in his book *The Value of Life* (1985), contemplates cases of extremely limited resources, such as choosing a patient for a single organ in a transplant program or a single spot in a renal dialysis program. As much as we might want to avoid ageism, he argues, we intuitively feel that something is wrong with offering a 95-year-old the same chance at these treatments as a 10-year-old or a 30-year-old. We believe that the younger person has not yet had a chance to experience what life has to offer. In his formulation of the fair innings argument, Harris argues that anyone below a threshold age (such as 70) should have equal priority for any life-saving medical treatment. Those who reach that threshold age have received their fair innings and have lower priority.

Harris' argument may seem extreme, but **fair innings ageism**, which explicitly or implicitly gives priority in health care to the young because of the belief that they have not yet had their fair chance at life, has strong common-sense appeal to many people. For example, Tsuchiya, Dolan, and Shaw (2003) present participants with a fictitious scenario. They tell the participants that each of five people (aged 5, 20, 35, 55, and 70) will die in a few days if they do not receive a medical treatment. When asked to specify the order in which these patients will be treated, the majority of the participants favor younger patients for fair innings reasons. They might say, for instance, that "The 5-year old has lived less life and deserves a chance" (p. 692). In a way, the fair innings argument has strong common-sense appeal despite its overt ageism.

The Case of Palliative Care

The utilitarian ageism of QALY maximization and other similar approaches is common in health economics, while fair innings ageism is common in medical ethics. On the face of it, it makes sense that we choose treatments that can allow the greatest number of quality years of life, and give priority to the young when it comes to life-saving treatments. But palliative care in particular fares poorly under either of these logics. Under the QALY-maximization logic, palliative care does not add years of life and, although it may add to the quality of remaining life, it is typically not enough to compare to life-saving treatments (Hughes, 2005). Under the fair innings logic, palliative care fares poorly because it expends resources on the elderly who are beyond the threshold age, rather than on younger people who have not yet had their fair innings. To the extent that we incorporate the fair innings argument or the QALY-maximization logic in our medical decision making, palliative care options are likely to be limited as they do not fare well under either approach. This has led some writers to propose alternatives for palliative care, such as the Palliative Care Yardstick (Normand, 2009), but these alternative approaches have not gained enough support to become commonplace.

The Chronosystem: The Medicalization of Aging

The chronosystem refers to changes over time in the individual's environment. These changes can occur on any level. For instance, a change of medical care provider or home address occurs at the level of the microsystem, but can be aspects of the chronosystem. In this chapter, rather than focus on changes in micro or mesosystems, we focus on historical changes in an aspect of the macrosystem that has occurred over the lifetimes of today's existing population of older adults: the medicalization of aging.

In the example above, the physician describes a palliative care unit, but does not mention the possibility of the patient dying at home. It is easy to forget that in the past, the vast majority of people died at home rather than in hospitals. Similarly, a century ago most babies in the United States were born at home. Today, fewer than 1 in 50 children are born at home (MacDorman, Matthews, & Declercq, 2014). Death, childbirth, and a host of other human problems have undergone a gradual process of **medicalization**, "defining a problem in medical terms, using medical language to describe a problem, adopting a medical framework to understand a problem, or using a medical intervention to 'treat' it" (Conrad, 1992, p. 211). The human problems that accompany "normal aging," such as limitations in physical ability and memory changes, have increasingly been defined as a series of illnesses and diseases to be cured or solved. For instance, prescription medications such as Viagra have become widespread largely by lowering the treatment thresholds of the problems they target and redefining conditions once considered part of normal aging as medical problems (Conrad, 2005). In a worst-case scenario, we start to view the elderly person as a pile of symptoms, illnesses, and pathologies.

Medicalization in the United States differs from medicalization in most other developed nations in that it leans on acute conditions, or medical conditions with a sudden onset. We use the term **acute medicalization** to describe this process, which depends largely on the Medicare Act of 1965. Because Medicare was designed as an acute-care program, medical services for older adults needed to be framed as the result of acute conditions to be considered for reimbursement, even if we might otherwise have considered these problems part of long-term or chronic care. Home care, for instance, fell under the jurisdiction of medical professionals who defined it as an extension of acute care. In contrast, social policy in Europe defined in-home care for the elderly as an extension of the Social Security system, rather than a response to a particular medical condition (Binney, Estes, & Ingman, 1990). For the purposes of Medicare reimbursement, old age is not just a series of medical conditions, but a series of acute medical conditions.

How (Un)-Ageist Can Health Care Be? The Power of Proximal Processes

Using Bronfenbrenner's ecological model of human development, we have examined the fictitious anecdote to reveal how ageism operates at six different levels: the individual, the microsystem, the mesosystem, the exosystem, the macrosystem, and the chronosystem. Despite the range of these systems, they all work through face-to-face interactions between the patient, the nurse, his daughter, and the physician. These processes have real power to shape the patient's continued development.

Based on this, we might argue that no matter the stereotypes that the individual patient brings with them, health care should strive to be truly age-neutral. And in fact, some forms of ageism in health care are easy to condemn, and interventions might reduce them substantially. In one intervention, Williams et al. (2017) used scripted PowerPoint presentations and handouts to raise consciousness about elderspeak in a series of three Changing Talk sessions. The talks, provided once a week over the course of three weeks, targeted nursing home staff. To evaluate the intervention, they used video recordings of interactions between the nursing home staff and patients with dementia, collected both before and after the intervention. They found that the intervention helped to improve communication and reduce how resistive patients were to care. Their intervention showed that, while elderspeak might be difficult to eliminate from health care entirely, its negative effects far outweighed any positive effects.

Other manifestations of ageism in health care are more ambiguous. For instance, we might argue against defining old age in terms of medical problems, but medicalization has carried with it numerous benefits for the elderly. For example, it has allowed for the successful treatment of a host of problems that might otherwise be considered part of "normal aging." Rather than considering lingering pain from an injury as part of normal aging ("the body just doesn't heal like it used to"), an elderly patient today might participate in physical therapy. Some conditions, such as pain and depression, might actually be *under*medicalized among the elderly, leaving treatable diseases undiagnosed. Drawing the line between good and bad medicalization is difficult.

The examples of elderspeak and medicalization draw attention to the continuum of acceptability that ageism in health care spans. Some forms may be completely unacceptable. Others we might reluctantly accept. Still others like ageism in triadic interactions may be difficult to target. Hence, we might be tempted to decry ageism of any type in health care, but it is perhaps among the most difficult social institution to make truly age-neutral.

Conclusion

In this chapter, we used the ecological model of human development to argue that ageism in health care exists at all levels of a person's environment. We then addressed ways in which ageism can affect experiences of health care at the levels of the individual, microsystem, mesosystem, exosystem, macrosystem, and chronosystem. We concluded by reflecting on how un-ageist health care can really be.

Discussion Questions

1 Consider the case of the single spot in the renal dialysis program, as Harris (1985) presents in his fair innings argument. (a) Choose between giving a 10-year-old or 100-year-old that spot. (b) Then, choose between a 30-year-old and a 40-year-old. Discuss your logic for each choice.
2 The short, fictitious example at the beginning of this chapter included numerous types and levels of ageism. Reimagine the example eliminating various elements of ageism (e.g., a triadic interaction without marginalization of the elderly adult). Which types of ageism are most difficult to eliminate?
3 The medicalization of aging, by redefining aging as a medical problem rather than a "human problem," may lead to older adults spending

more time in the doctor's office, but is it a bad thing? Discuss the pros and cons of the medicalization of aging.
4. Daniel Callahan (1995) argues that the aims of medicine should be saving lives for those before a certain threshold age (whether the late 70s or early 80s) and alleviating pain and suffering for patients over that age. Does this argument make sense to you? Why or why not?

7 Peripheral Ageism in Employment

From Explanation to Action

Imagine a student a few months away from college graduation. He writes well and understands social media, so he begins searching online job postings for social media, technical, and content writer positions. He quickly grows discouraged, as most entry-level jobs require years of experience. How will he get experience if he cannot get a job, and how will he get a job if he does not have experience?

This example, while hypothetical, is a persistent problem for younger workers. For instance, one recent analysis finds that over half of job postings in technical writing list a bachelor's degree as a characteristic of the ideal candidate, over three quarters list one or more years of existing job experience, and many list both a degree and experience (Brumberger & Lauer, 2015). Since this is a combination that new college graduates are unlikely to have had an opportunity to accrue, they are at a disadvantage relative to those already established in the labor force. On the other end of the age distribution, older workers experience parallel problems (AARP, 2014). In spite of legislation designed to protect them, about 20 percent say that they have personally experienced age discrimination in employment (Benz et al., 2013). Labor market statistics back up this picture of bifurcated disadvantage. Overall, the unemployed are disproportionately aged in their early 20s, but both younger workers and older workers are more likely to be unemployed for 26 weeks or longer than those in middle-age (Monge-Naranjo & Sohail, 2015). Age discrimination in the labor market cuts both ways, while leaving the middle comparatively untouched.

In this chapter, we use the term **peripheral ageism** to describe a pattern of ageism in which the middle-aged are the advantaged group. As shown in Figure 7.1, perceived age discrimination tends to be highest among younger and older workers (Snape & Redman, 2003), although it can take on different aspects depending on the age of the person and the workplace context. Prejudice and discrimination in employment can occur in day-to-day workplace interactions, in promotion and advancement decisions, in firings and layoffs, and in a host of other ways. However, many of these examples, such as the speed of a person's promotion to different positions, are difficult to research and quantify because they require inside knowledge of each

Figure 7.1 Peripheral ageism in the workplace

organization. Other examples, such as layoffs, occur only for some organizations and predominantly in some industries, making it difficult to draw conclusions among ageism overall. In this chapter, to avoid some of these complications, we instead begin with the issue of hiring-related decisions, such as whether a resume gets a call-back, whether a person gets an interview, and whether a candidate gets a job offer.

Underlying this chapter is a question that goes beyond ageism: How do underlying explanations of phenomena such as diversity and prejudice influence what actions we can and should take? Put more simply, how do we get from explanation to action? In the first part of this chapter, we discuss aspects of prejudice and discrimination in work and employment in the context of five potential explanations. In the second part of the chapter, we consider how each explanation of peripheral ageism influences what actions we might take to try to reduce ageism in the workplace based on each of these explanations. Our understanding of ageism influences what actions we think we can—and should—take to reduce it. The wrong assumptions about the causes of ageism might lead us to choose a course of action that is ineffectual or, at worst, exacerbates the problem by magnifying prejudice over time.

Understanding Peripheral Ageism

Below, we discuss the five following explanations for peripheral ageism (Figure 7.2): (1) the overlapping prejudices explanation, which posits that peripheral ageism represents the coexistence of ageism, which puts older adults at a disadvantage, and reverse ageism, which puts younger adults at a disadvantage; (2) the cognitive processes explanation, which explains peripheral ageism as the result of normal psychological processes; (3) the incomplete authority shift explanation, which views peripheral ageism as the

Peripheral Ageism in Employment 97

Explanations for peripheral ageism in work and employment

Practices to reduce peripheral ageism would...

Ageism and reverse ageism have separate explanations → 1. Overlapping prejudices →

... target prejudice and discrimination equally
* *reduce prejudice against older workers*
* *reduce discrimination against younger workers*

Ageism and reverse ageism share an explanation →
- 2. Cognitive processes
  - 2a. In-group/Out-group
  - 2b. Statistical discrimination

reduce in-group/out-group bias

use HR policies to combat discrimination

- 3. Incomplete authority shift →
- 4. Frame analysis
  - 4a. Ideal worker frame
  - 4b. Ideal career frame
- 5. Intersectionality

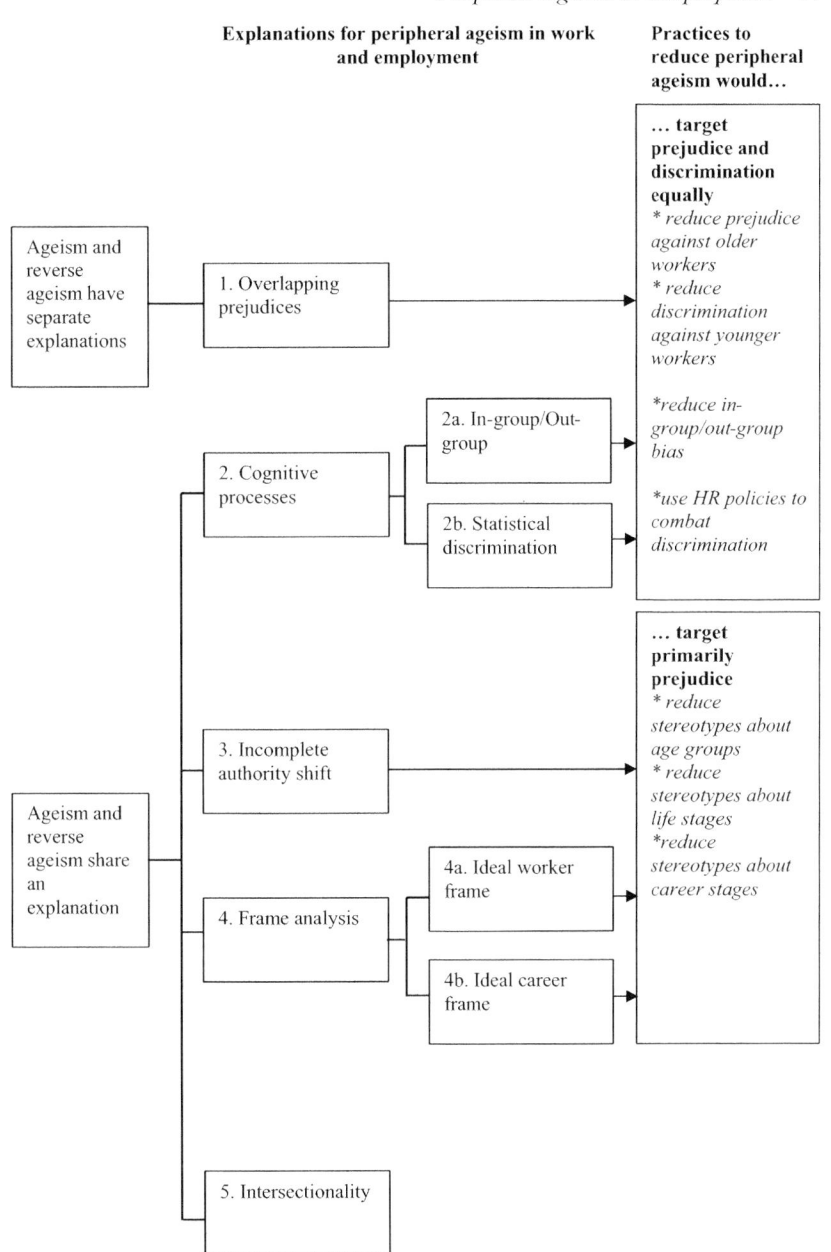

... target primarily prejudice
* *reduce stereotypes about age groups*
* *reduce stereotypes about life stages*
* *reduce stereotypes about career stages*

Figure 7.2 Explanations for peripheral ageism in work and employment

result of a partial shift from traditional to secular-rational orientations to authority; (4) the frame analysis explanation, which sees peripheral ageism as the result of the deviance of workers from the ideal worker and ideal career frames; and (5) the intersectionality explanation, which posits that peripheral ageism depends partly on other aspects of diversity, such as race, gender, and ethnicity. The first of these (overlapping prejudices) is unique in that it assumes that peripheral ageism does not have a single, unitary cause. Instead, prejudice against the old and prejudice against the young might have two distinct causes.

Two Age Groups, Two Reasons: The Overlapping Prejudices Explanation

The results of some studies that look at discrimination in hiring against older adults and younger adults separately would suggest that peripheral ageism represents the coexistence of prejudices against the old and against the young. From this perspective, each prejudice has its own underlying logic, but they appear as a single "peripheral ageism."

Discrimination against Older Adults

Research on discrimination against older adults in hiring often uses **audit studies**, in which fictional interviewees are coached to act identically but have different demographic characteristics, or **correspondence studies**, in which fictional resumes are identical in terms of qualifications but differ in easily discernible demographic characteristics (Neumark, 2010). For instance, an audit study addressing gender discrimination might compare hiring outcomes for two resumes: both with identical educational credentials and experience, but one with an obviously female name (e.g., Jacqueline) and one with an obviously male name (e.g., Thomas). In one study of age discrimination, economist Joanna Lahey (2008) sent fictional resumes to almost 4,000 firms located around Boston, Massachusetts and Saint Petersburg, Florida. She used a computer program to generate pairs of resumes that were identical in all ways, except the date of high school graduation. Employers could infer the approximate age of her fictional applicants by the year that they graduated from high school (making them ages 35, 45, 50, 55, and 62). She found that fictional applicants aged 35 or 45 were about 40 percent more likely to be asked to a job interview than were fictional applicants aged 50, 55, or 62. In Boston, a 35-year-old woman applying for a job could expect one interview for every 19 resumes she submitted. A 55-year-old woman with identical qualifications would need to file 23 applications. The Saint Petersburg figures were similar, a disheartening prospect since Lahey deliberately chose Saint Petersburg as a city whose current age distribution mirrored the future age distribution of the United States as a whole. The persistence of age discrimination in this aging labor market suggested that, as the population of the United States aged, hiring decisions would not necessarily become less ageist.

Even when older adults got an interview, they faced another hurdle. Their faces could give away their age in a way that activated stereotypes of lower fitness and poorer health. An older appearance often proved to be a more serious detriment than an older chronological age in the interview process (Kaufmann, Krings, & Sczesny, 2016). This created pressure for older job applicants to look young, even if the years of graduation listed on their resumes provided evidence of their "real" ages. Some older job applicants deliberately concealed the physical, material, and social signs of aging. Both men and women dyed their hair, wore youthful clothes, and used "younger" language in preparation for interviews. As one 58-year-old woman put it, when job interviews were concerned "the one thing you need[ed was] your bottle of dye" (Berger, 2009: 327). Older adults faced hurdles in hiring and selection beginning as early as their 50s.

Discrimination against Younger Adults

Audit and correspondence studies, such as Lahey's (2008), have generally not addressed the problems of workers in their early to mid-20s. There is a simple, logistical reason that audit studies may be less effective for these age groups. Most human resource managers look at work history up to ten years in the past, so to generate fictional resumes with equivalent amounts of experience, the youngest believable ages are between 28 (for high school-educated fictional workers) and 32 (for college-educated fictional workers). This means that many extensive studies dealing with hiring discrimination exclude workers younger than their 30s.

Other sources of information suggest that underemployment is a major hurdle that younger adults face. Over half of 22-year-old college graduates are underemployed, working in jobs that do not require a college education. The rate of underemployment for new college graduates fluctuates depending on economic conditions. In recent decades, the types of jobs that people are underemployed in have worsened. That is, good non-college jobs do not require a college education and represent underemployment for college-educated workers, but they are relatively stable and well paid. These include positions such as dental hygienist or electrician, which allow a person to support themselves, offer some limited chance for advancement, and typically offer benefits as well. Bad non-college jobs, on the other hand, include entry-level retail positions or janitorial work, have average annual wages of under $25,000, offer little stability, and provide almost no chance of advancement. While underemployment rates among new college graduates are similar today to those in the early 1990s, the proportion of bad jobs relative to good jobs among those who are unemployed has increased (Abel, Deitz, & Su, 2014). One explanation is the difficulty of breaking into fields requiring college education. As the demand for new pools of certain cognitive skills wanes, many more people have college degrees focusing on those skills than the labor market needs (Beaudry, Green, & Sand, 2014, 2016). Over time, people stop gravitating toward oversupplied skill sets. However, the general practice of treating number of years of experience as a proxy for ability means that, whenever new graduates have to compete with established workers in fields with oversupplied skill sets, the younger workers bear the brunt of the mismatch.

What Explains Peripheral Ageism: Overlapping Prejudices

Taken at face value, peripheral ageism might appear to be largely the product of two separate ageisms. First, older adults face ageism based on stereotypes about lower fitness or health. Second, younger adults face reverse ageism because they are most at risk when their skill set is oversupplied in the labor market. Because the combined effects of the two ageisms are at their lowest points for middle-aged workers, we might decide that peripheral ageism is really the result of two separate prejudices. This explanation is appealing on the surface, but is it really the whole story? A piecemeal approach requires a separate explanation not only for age groups but also for each facet of employment. For instance, promotion decisions among already hired workers cannot be due to the difficulty of breaking into new fields among younger workers.

The remaining four explanations attempt to explain peripheral ageism as a single phenomenon, in which prejudices against the young and against the old have the same core reason in various work contexts. The first of these, the cognitive processes explanation, considers prejudice the result of normal psychological processes that would extend to various realms of work and life.

The Logical Conclusion? The Cognitive Processes Explanation

Stereotype processes, described in more detail in Chapter 1, focus on the mechanisms through which prejudice and discrimination are created and perpetuated. Below, we consider two types of stereotype processes (in-group/out-group bias and statistical discrimination) as potential explanations for peripheral ageism. Both approaches explain peripheral ageism as the result of normal cognitive processes that favor the middle-aged at the expense of both younger and older adults.

In-Group/Out-Group Bias

What if peripheral ageism in hiring stems from a tendency to feel hostility toward out-groups and favoritism toward in-groups? Experiments such as Robber's Cave (Sherif, 1958) demonstrate that people will favor in-groups over out-groups, even if the definitions of the in-group are highly superficial. And theorists such as Tajfel and Turner (1979) suggest that real material advantages (e.g., money, prestige) are not always the key good at stake. People have innate needs for self-esteem, and if they view in-groups ("people like me") as superior to out-groups ("people unlike me"), they have, by extension, defined themselves as superior and deserving of esteem.

For example, you might believe that people who like Musician A are better than those who like Musician B. If you like Musician A, then by definition you are superior in musical taste to those who like Musician B.

Divisions between in-groups and out-groups play out on all levels of a person's life, but in the workplace people are less likely to be able to create in-groups based on deep similarities such as similarity of core beliefs and values. We generally know less about the personal lives and beliefs of our co-workers than of our friends and family, but because work is such an important part of our lives we may still seek to define and then favor in-groups. In such cases, surface-level demographic similarities such as gender and race can become the basis for preferences. Research in relational demography (Tsui & O'Reilly, 1989) has found that aspects of demographic similarity, including gender (Choi, 2007) and race (Avey, West, & Crossley, 2008), provide a basis for prejudice. Relational demography is an extension of social identity theory, discussed in Chapter 1. We assume that co-workers who are similar to us in age, race, and gender are more like us in deep-level ways than those who are different from us, and then we favor those in-groups over out-groups. For instance, in the case of gender, men might view themselves as the in-group and women as the out-group.

For age, the definition of the in-group and out-group is fuzzier. A 50-year-old worker could see the "in-group" as other 50-year-old workers, but consider 40-year-old workers and 60-year-old workers to be more similar to them than 20-year-old workers or 70-year-old workers. That is, relative age might involve the creation of what we call **near out-groups** (or alternatively, **near in-groups**) that we view more favorably than true out-groups but less favorably than true in-groups. In a workplace with younger, middle-aged, and older workers, older workers would have the least negatively ageist attitudes toward other older workers (in-group), and the most negatively ageist attitudes toward younger workers (out-group), with middle-aged workers considered a near out-group. Younger workers would be least negatively ageist toward other younger workers, and most negatively ageist toward older workers. Overall perceived ageism, in the form of negative attitudes from people of each age, would be at its lowest point for middle-aged workers.

One weakness of in-groups and out-groups as an explanation for peripheral ageism is that the evidence for the effects of age dissimilarity, as compared to gender and race dissimilarity, is inconsistent. Some research has found that people prefer their own age group, but the preference is slight (Goldberg, Riordan, & Schaffer, 2010; Van der Heijden et al., 2010). It is still possible that age may serve as a basis for workplace bias, but the strength of its effect may be too low to account for peripheral ageism by itself.

Imperfect Knowledge in Hiring

Another explanation for peripheral ageism looks at the cognitive reasons behind discrimination, rather than those behind prejudice. Employers believe that age correlates with various job-related characteristics, often for good reason. For instance, younger workers tend to have fewer soft skills, such as project management skills, simply because they have had less experience in a given field. Older workers tend to have fewer physical advantages, particularly those related to strenuous jobs, because of age-related increases in disability. Based on age alone, an employer cannot determine whether a given younger worker lacks particular skills, or whether a given older worker cannot meet the demands of the job. However, the stronger the presumed relationship between age and the desired attribute (being a "digital native," having "wisdom"), the more that employers are likely to substitute group averages ("Most Millennials are digital natives") for individual characteristics ("This Millennial is a digital native"). This type of statistical discrimination, which we discussed in more detail in Chapter 1, while more often applied to race and gender (Phelps, 1972; Arrow, 1973), might offer a unified way of understanding peripheral ageism. Older and younger workers alike are victims of employers' imperfect knowledge of individual attributes. The age at which statistical discrimination is least likely to hold sway is middle-age, when physical declines are generally less pronounced but education and initial years of experience are already in place.

Statistical discrimination is not always what we might consider "real" discrimination, however. Scholes (2014) points out that, in some cases, statistical discrimination may be unethical because it is demeaning to individual capabilities. For instance, suppose that we know that smokers are slightly less productive than non-smokers. Hiring a non-smoker over a smoker may be statistical discrimination, but the tenuous link between smoking and lower productivity makes that discrimination unfair. On the other hand, suppose we know that people with an engineering degree and several years of engineering experience are more productive as engineers than those who lack these attributes. Choosing a job candidate with a degree and experience over a job candidate without those attributes may be statistical discrimination (Baumle & Fossett, 2005), yet not be unfair because the criteria link directly to the job (Scholes, 2014). The same may apply to older workers, particularly those applying for jobs with physical demands.

What Explains Peripheral Ageism: Cognitive Processes

Relational demography and statistical discrimination share a core feature: they view peripheral ageism as a response to normal psychological needs and processes. In the case of relative age, a need for self-esteem drives us to prefer people who are similar to us, and in the workplace we are likely to rely on surface-level similarities such as age, race, and gender. In the case of statistical discrimination, we respond to imperfect knowledge by substituting group-level characteristics for individual-level characteristics.

One problem with using cognitive processes as the sole explanation for discrimination in employment is that it is largely ahistorical. Depending on cultural and historical circumstances, middle-aged adults have not always had advantages over younger and older adults. Below, we offer an alternative explanation for peripheral ageism in employment based on larger cultural shifts.

Times Are Changing: The Incomplete Authority Shift Explanation

Value modernization theory (discussed in Chapter 2) suggests that level of development is associated with two general trends: (1) an authority shift, in which the dominant societal values shift from traditional to secular-rational and (2) a well-being shift, in which the dominant societal values shift from survival to self-expression (Inglehart & Welzel, 2005). Within this framework, societies vary substantially because of unique historical and cultural circumstances.

Orientation to Authority

Many of the stereotypes relevant to the workplace map on to a historical shift in orientations to authority from traditional (in which older adults are the guardians of tradition) to secular-rational (in which traditional authority is devalued relative to other sources), but the level of economic development and values are only imperfectly linked. Due to unique historical and cultural contexts, most affluent English-speaking countries, including the United States, fall midway between traditional and secular-rational values, despite their high scores on self-expression values and their high levels of economic development (Inglehart & Welzel, 2005). The coexistence of two sets of orientations to authority may help to explain the prevalence of peripheral ageism in these countries.

Consistent with a traditional orientation toward authority, stereotypes or perceptions of younger workers include lower dependability (Posthuma & Campion, 2009) and less conscientious in general (Truxillo, McCune, Bertolino, & Fraccaroli, 2012). Younger workers are less likely to be viewed as embodying traditional work values or as having established wisdom. Consistent with a secular-rational orientation to authority, stereotypes or perceptions of older workers include resistance to change, lower adaptability, difficulties learning from training (Posthuma & Campion, 2009), lower fluid intelligence, and less proactive personalities (Truxillo et al., 2012). This set of stereotypes affects not only hiring, but also other aspects of employment such as employers' willingness to invest in training.

What Explains Peripheral Ageism: The Incomplete Authority Shift

The incomplete authority shift explanation posits that peripheral ageism will be highest in cultures where traditional and secular-rational values have substantial presence. In cultures with highly traditional values, older adults will be revered. In cultures with highly secular-rational values, younger adults will have an advantage. But in cultures such as the English-speaking developed countries, in which traditional and secular-rational orientations toward authority have almost equal strength, both older and younger workers are the targets of prejudice.

One weakness of the incomplete authority shift as an explanation for peripheral ageism is that it largely ignores the role of individual and group agency. Certain organizations have adopted practices that directly support positive views of younger workers, older workers, or both (Center on Aging and Work, n.d.), while other organizations have not. Below, we offer an alternative explanation for peripheral ageism based on frame analysis, which suggests that while overall cultural frames might support peripheral ageism, counter frames are possible.

Response to Deviance: The Frame Analysis Explanation

Frame analysis, described in more detail in Chapter 3, looks at prejudice and discrimination as largely the product of which frames, or ways of understanding and organizing experience, prevail (Goffman, 1974). Below, we consider two frames, the ideal worker frame and the ideal career frame, as potential explanations for peripheral ageism. Both frames arose from labor market conditions near the turn of the nineteenth century, and both frames could indirectly generate ageism by defining older and younger workers as deviants from workplace frames.

The Ideal Worker Frame: Women and Older Workers

In *Unbending Gender*, legal scholar Joan Williams (1999) argued that, by the turn of the nineteenth century, labor market conditions promoted a model in which men worked outside the home while women worked inside the home. Employers expected the ideal worker to dedicate himself to his job to the almost complete exclusion of family caregiving responsibilities. In line with Williams' arguments, the **ideal worker frame** was a way of understanding and organizing work around a hypothetical "ideal worker," a typically male worker who put in long hours at work and maintained a sharp division between work and family. The frame disproportionately punished women because they were often unable to fully devote themselves to the workplace. For instance, sociologist Mary Blair-Loy (2005), in *Competing Devotions*, argued that the marginalization of women as caregivers was detrimental to women's careers because work was structured in such a way that it punished those with family responsibilities.

As Williams (1999) has noted, the separation of workers into "mothers and others" (p. 2) creates a pattern of harm that goes beyond women. For example, older workers might also find themselves the target of prejudice and discrimination because they often want flexible schedules, to downshift from their work responsibilities, or to shift into bridge jobs. These needs and preferences directly contradict the ideal worker frame (Matz-Costa, 2012), and the deviance of certain categories of workers from the ideal worker frame represents a potentially concealable stigma, "an attribute that is deeply discrediting" (Goffman, 1963, p. 3). Because the structure of the workplace requires that people embrace the ideal worker frame to reap certain social rewards such as promotions (Brumley, 2014), people often attempt to pass as members of the favored (ideal worker) group (Reid, 2015). However, because older workers and women are disproportionately likely to be "non-ideal" workers, they are more likely to be the targets of prejudice and discrimination due to others' perceptions that they do not quite fit the ideal (e.g., they spend too much time caring for children, or they are not ambitious enough in taking on new work responsibilities).

The Ideal Career Myth: Younger and Older Workers

A second frame links the ideal worker frame to age, putting younger and older workers alike at a disadvantage. We refer to this as the **ideal career frame**, the idea of a linear career, in which workers begin at the bottom of the hierarchy, work to establish themselves in their organization, and then disengage from work. This frame creates a timetable or a set of norms and expectations about when workers are expected to take on and leave various responsibilities (Lashbrook, 1996).

In human resource management, **career development theory** provides a formal articulation of the ideal career frame. According to theorists such as Donald Super (1990), a career—"the individually perceived sequence of attitudes and behaviors associated with work-related behaviors and activities over the span of the person's life" (Hall, 2002, p. 12)—reflects a series of successive developmental tasks related to individual self-concept. Individuals try to align and develop their self-concept through various roles, of which career is only one. Stages include growth, in which individuals develop their initial interests and abilities; exploration, in which they make their first choices regarding occupation and enter the labor force; establishment, in which they pursue a fit between their jobs and preferences, needs, and skills; maintenance, in which they try to reach and maintain their highest performance within their careers; and disengagement, in which they reduce or cease work. Career stage theorists generally link career stages to age (Super, 1990; Hall, 2002) and, to the extent that career stage theory links maintenance to middle-aged workers, it defines the middle-aged as the most likely to be currently fulfilling their potential.

What Explains Peripheral Ageism: Frame Analysis

Based on frame analysis, two closely related frames, the ideal worker and ideal career frames, explain peripheral ageism in hiring. The ideal worker frame discourages employers from hiring older workers, who may not want to or be able to devote themselves to the workplace fully. The ideal career frame means that employers view middle-aged workers as reaching and maintaining their highest performance. Implicit in the ideal worker frame is the issue of intersectionality. The ideal worker is not just a person who dedicates themselves to the job, he is typically a male worker. Below, we look at the question of peripheral ageism from the perspective of intersectionality between age and other aspects of social inequality such as gender.

Legal Manifestations of Peripheral Ageism: The Intersectionality Explanation

Intersectionality, discussed in more detail in Chapter 4, deals with the connection of various forms of prejudice and discrimination, based on factors such as age, gender, and race. Below, we consider the gendered life course as a facet of peripheral ageism. The emphasis in this section is how laws and regulations can have subtle effects on ageism, but intersectionality can also occur in other facets of prejudice and discrimination.

Gendered Ageism: Older Women Fare Worse?

The fictional resumes that Lahey used in her 2008 study were solely for women, because she was interested in entry-level positions such as secretarial and cashier positions for which older men would seldom apply. Neumark, Burn, and Button (2016), in a recent study including 40,000 fictional applicants, instead included both female and male applicants by selecting a wider range of occupations, including administration, sales, and janitorial jobs. As shown in Figure 7.3, the call-back rates were sharply different for younger as opposed to older women in both administrative and sales positions. About 29 percent of younger women applying for a sales job received a call-back, compared to 18 percent of older women. But for men, the differences between older and younger men were much less pronounced. About 21 percent of younger men received call-backs for sales positions, compared to 15 percent of older men. When the researchers considered other factors such as specific skills listed on resumes (e.g., number of words typed per minute), the evidence for age discrimination remained strong for women, but weak or non-existent for men.

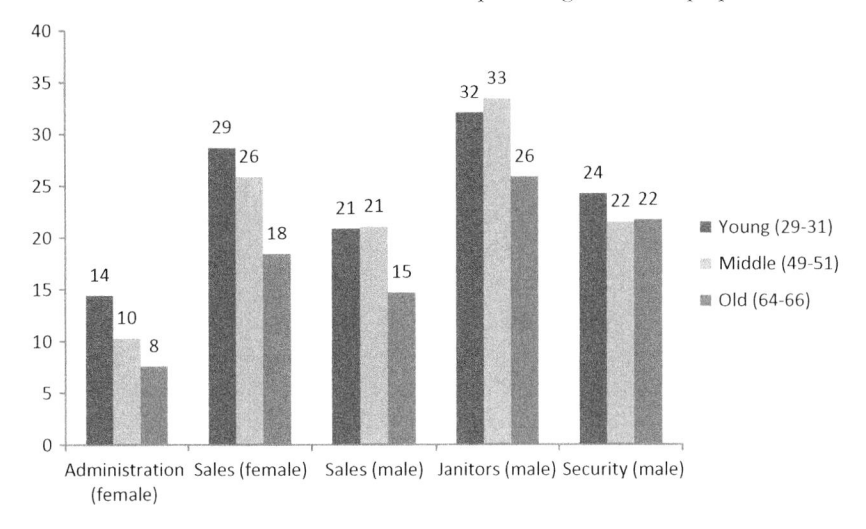

Figure 7.3 Rates of call-backs
Source: Neumark, Burn, & Button, 2016

Neumark et al. (2016)'s evidence for discrimination in hiring women was consistent across a wide range of cities, ranging from those with stronger state age-discrimination laws and an older age distribution (Miami) to weaker discrimination laws and a younger age distribution (Salt Lake City). They proposed two related explanations. First, people judged women harshly more based on appearance and perceived women's appearance as declining more rapidly with age. Hence, the disadvantages that existed for women, relative to men, grew with age. Second, and equally important, the laws that might otherwise protect older women were inadequate due to the historical circumstances of their adoption. The two dimensions of inequality (age and gender) were covered under two separate laws, adopted at separate times. Title VII of the Civil Rights Act protected women from discrimination based on gender, and the ADEA protected older workers. Court cases brought under Title VII generally failed on the grounds that older women were not a separate protected class. Court cases brought under the ADEA generally failed because courts ruled that subgroup protections were not covered under the ADEA (Song, 2013; Day, 2014). In the case of older women and hiring, the lack of legal recognition of intersectionality between age and other dimensions of inequality perpetuated a system of cumulative inequality. Older women who were targets of discrimination both relative to older men and younger women had only the shakiest legal protections.

What Explains Peripheral Ageism: Intersectionality

Intersectionality encourages us to look closely at how age intersects with other aspects of inequality. Women tend to suffer more from age discrimination, both due to stereotypes about physical appearance and because of the way that laws in the United States are currently structured. Intersectionality is compatible with other explanations but does not stand on its own well. It does not tell us about the basic mechanisms of ageism, but primarily how those mechanisms differ depending on other dimensions of inequality.

From Explanation to Action

We often implicitly believe we should not only celebrate diversity, but that we should use it as an asset in organizations. But, diversity is a double-edged sword. Work groups that are diverse tend to benefit because people bring different information and cognitive styles to the table, but those benefits can come at substantial costs in terms of outcomes such as group integration (Milliken & Martins, 1996). Put more simply, people in diverse groups work better in the short term, but they don't like each other much and that has serious costs for individuals and organizations in the long term. Employers who want to forge diversity into "a single-edged sword" (Boehm & Swertmann, 2015), getting the benefits of diversity without the disadvantages, often start by attempting to reduce prejudice and discrimination. Below, as shown in Figure 7.2, we argue that the five explanations we have described above suggest two different pathways to reduce ageism and age discrimination in the workplace: one that focuses on prejudice first and one that focuses on discrimination first.

The Prejudice-First Approach

If we accept the incomplete authority shift or frame analysis explanation, we consider underlying prejudices the core problem. In the case of the incomplete authority shift, the main areas of prejudice are the stereotypes of older workers as inflexible or inadaptable (as in the secular-rational orientation to authority) and of younger workers as unreliable or as having poor work ethics (as in the traditional orientation to authority). In the case of the ideal worker frame, the main areas of prejudice are negative stereotypes about workers at life stages with substantial family responsibilities, such as childcare or eldercare. In the case of the ideal career stage frame, the main areas of prejudice deal with the definition of early and late career workers as less productive or worthwhile than mid-career workers.

Evidence seems to back up the importance of reducing stereotypes. For instance, in a 2013 study of over 300 German workers aged 19 to 64 years, researchers Catherine Bowen and Ursula Staudinger studied how much of older workers' declining interest in promotion was due to ageism. They found that older workers who believed that their team perceived older workers negatively were less interested in promotion than were older workers who believed that their team perceived older workers positively. Other studies have shown similar results: age stereotypes make the management of diversity more difficult and less successful (Dordoni & Argentero, 2015). The "prejudice-first approach"—trying to reduce stereotypes and bias through methods such as diversity training—seems like common sense, yet there is less than certain evidence that diversity training is worth its huge price tag. It is difficult to train people away from their prejudices, because those prejudices are ingrained and often implicit. Previous research on gender and race diversity training suggests that such training can even backfire (Dobbin, Kalev, & Kelly, 2007). Employees required to undergo training for diversity can feel resentment toward the very groups that the training attempted to help. This has led some companies away from diversity training, and toward other approaches that focus less on prejudice, and more on practice.

The Discrimination-First Approach

Several of the explanations that we discussed would lead to a focus on practices first, even if changing underlying attitudes was a secondary effect. For instance, the overlapping prejudices explanation and the cognitive processes explanation suggest that some facets of age discrimination can be short-circuited by careful human resource practices, such as reducing language about number of years' experience in job descriptions.

A host of employer practices designed to respond to the aging workforce also indirectly reduce discrimination between age groups through one of two means: age-specific practices aimed to fill gaps for certain age groups and age-neutral practices that build bridges across generations, age groups, or career stages. The primary aim of these programs, such as reverse mentoring in which younger workers mentor older workers, is seldom to reduce stereotypes. However, they often are more successful than the common diversity training approach (Dobbin et al., 2007). Box 7.1 gives two examples of age-specific practices, each of which aims to fill gaps in career development and networking for different generations. Box 7.2 describes a reverse mentoring program which aims to leverage the expertise of early-career workers. Both approaches do little to address prejudice directly, but may have indirect effects on prejudice levels over time. Box 7.2, in particular, fits closely with explanations that see both prejudice and discrimination as important to combat.

Box 7.1 Case Studies: The Divide and Conquer Approach

The following two employee-run programs take a similar approach to issues of age. They recognize that the age groups (or career stages or generations) have different needs and priorities, and then address those priorities in age-specific groups. The aim of this approach is to ensure that all employees, regardless of age, have access to resources for employee development and work-life balance. Key features of both programs include a focus on career stage or generation rather than on age, and the use of employee leadership.

Glaxo-Smith-Kline, a large multinational pharmaceutical company, implemented two networking groups run by employee members in 2006 and 2007:

- **The Early Career Network** focused on networking among employees in early career, but was open to all employees. Priorities included building employees' personal support networks in the workplace.
- **The Prime Time Partners** focused on networking among employees in mid-career and later, but was open to all employees. Topics included career development.

The early pilot groups had a membership of 50 employees, but later enrolled approximately 800 members. Over 90 percent of the members were satisfied with the programs.

Wells Fargo, a large multinational financial services company, launched a series of networking groups for employees:

- **Boomers Network** (Boomers, born between 1946 and 1964).
- **Young Professional Network group** (Millennials, born 1981–2000 and GenXers, born 1965–80).

Topics of interest for both groups included retirement planning and networking.

Source: Center on Aging and Work Innovative Practices Database

Box 7.2 Case Studies: The Building Bridges Approach

The following program aimed primarily to help top leadership in the company leverage the technical and communications expertise of early-career employees. However, by creating a formal structure in which older and younger employees worked together directly, it indirectly lowered divisions between age groups.

Executives at **The Hartford**, a large financial service company, recognized that the insurance industry was changing in two major ways: customers were increasingly turning to the internet for insurance and financial advice, and the impending retirement of many Baby Boomers meant that business practices needed to adjust to a workforce increasingly dominated by Millennials. Their reverse mentoring program included:

- **Top leadership in the company**, including both the chairman of the company and leaders of the business units, as mentees.
- **Early-career employees** with technical and communication skills as mentors.

As a direct result of the program, mentors supported the revision of the company's electronic usage policy so that employees could use social media to do their work. As an indirect result, most of the mentees received promotions within one year because of the additional networking opportunities and organizational visibility associated with the program.

Source: Center on Aging and Work Innovative Practices Database

Explanation Matters

The explanation of peripheral ageism that we adopt influences what type of practices and policies we believe will reduce its negative effects. But it also influences the extent to which we think it really is possible to stamp out prejudice and discrimination. For instance, if we accept the frame analysis explanation of peripheral ageism, we will see the failure of diversity programs as evidence of the strength of existing cultural frames. If we instead accept the cognitive processes explanation, we focus on ways in which we can circumvent current practices so that cognitive processes (such as responses to incomplete knowledge) will not have significant effects on actual practice. In this vein, in Box 7.3 we discuss two programs that aim to recruit younger and older adults without addressing underlying stereotypes. If we believe that the correct target is discrimination first, these efforts are an effective first step. If we believe that the correct target is prejudice first, these efforts are illusory at best.

Box 7.3 Case Studies: Correcting Recruitment

The following two employers have instituted recruitment practices that specifically draw from pools of older and younger adults, respectively. The two programs, while they may seem different on the surface, share core features including: partnership with existing community organizations; development or identification of individuals with skill sets that the employers need; and a focus on older and younger adults, groups that are typically at a disadvantage in recruitment.

A medium-sized company providing home health services, **Renewal Care Partners** decided that the needs of their clients were best served by matching them with caregivers who were in tune with their backgrounds and interests. They partnered with various community organizations whose memberships were predominantly older adults, including

> the Actors Fund, local senior centers, and Services and Advocacy for GLBT Elders to advertise and recruit employees.
>
> A logistics and distribution company located in Greenville, South Carolina, **Grove Medical** partnered with the local school system to develop a program relevant to logistics and materials handling. Young adults graduating from high school had the opportunity to develop industry-specific skills as part of their course work.
>
> *Source*: Center on Aging and Work Innovative Practices Database and SHRM

Conclusion

In this chapter, we argue that peripheral ageism is the dominant type of ageism in employment, and we propose five potential explanations: overlapping prejudices, cognitive processes, incomplete authority shift, frame analysis, and intersectionality. We map the ways in which the chosen explanation can guide the potential actions to reduce peripheral ageism, providing a number of case studies of employer practices.

Discussion Questions

1 When you go to a job interview, you might take extra care with your clothing and appearance, but where would you draw the line? In one study, older job seekers who refused on principle to cater to ageism by attempting to appear younger were in the minority (Berger, 2009). Would you refuse on principle to present yourself as (a) older or younger, (b) a different race or ethnicity, or (c) a different gender than you are in an interview to get a job?

2 The potential for conflict between older workers and younger supervisors remains a topic of concern in the workplace (Collins, Hair, & Rocco, 2009), despite evidence that these concerns are often overstated. Using each of the five explanations, how would you explain the persistent stereotype that there is (or could be) conflict between older workers and younger supervisors?

3 Consider Box 7.3. Do you think that these practices—which ignore prejudice in favor of combatting discrimination—are more effective than trying to change underlying attitudes? If not, what employer practices would you suggest instead?

8 Three Ways to Use an Ideology
A Political Economy of Ageism

Imagine you receive an advertisement in the mail for a new community. The management of the community regularly sponsors parties and other activities. Because the housing units are small, the costs to rent or buy are reasonable. However, only households in which at least one member is age 55 or older can rent or buy in the community. You would probably give little thought to such an advertisement because these types of **age-restricted communities** are both widespread and legal in the United States. And despite their obvious discrimination against younger and middle-aged adults, there is little public debate questioning their ethics.

In light of our clear rejection of housing discrimination based on race, gender, and disability, why do we so readily accept age discrimination in housing? We argue in this chapter that our acceptance of a range of social and economic policies, including legislation surrounding age-restricted communities, rests in part on **ideologies** or frames. Ideologies and frames are two overlapping ideas from complementary perspectives within the social sciences. The term "ideology" originates in political economy, politics, and policy studies, while the term "frame" has roots in behavioral economics, psychology, and sociology. Both can have elements of ageism, and can foster or stymie public acceptance of discriminatory age-related policies. Aside from their origin, perhaps the greatest difference between the two concepts is one of perspective. Thinking in terms of political ideologies focuses attention on cultural reservoirs of ideas. Thinking in terms of frames focuses attention on the strips of experience that the frames highlight.

In Chapter 4, we discuss the role of frames in shaping public policy. In this chapter, we instead use the term "ideology" because of its connection with political economy, a theoretical perspective on the relationships between government, economics, and other systems of power. Gerontologist Caroll Estes (2001), in her model of the political economy of aging, outlines three ways in which individuals and groups use ideologies: in the creation of cultural images, in the formulation of appeals to the economic system, and in the implementation of systems of rational problem solving. We provide examples of how individuals and groups have used ideologies to support policies related to the aged in each of these ways, and discuss the

114 *Ageism in Context*

implications for the state and other systems of power. At the end of the chapter, we return to the question of age-restricted communities, arguing that public acceptance rests in part on the ideology of compassionate ageism.

The Political Economy of Aging: Insights from the Critical Tradition in Gerontology

As a field, **political economy**, the study of the connections between politics, economics, and other systems of power, has a long history. Many texts, such as Adam Smith's (1776) *Wealth of Nations* and John Stuart Mill's (1848) *Principles of Political Economy*, use the term political economy to refer to what we now consider economics or politics. While the separation of economics and politics into two fields has reduced interest in political economy as a field in itself (Drazen, 2000), political economy as a perspective within the social sciences has experienced a rebirth due in part to its connection with the critical perspective of the Frankfurt School.

The Critical Perspective: The Legacy of the Frankfurt School

The **Frankfurt School**, a school of philosophical and social thought, originated at Frankfurt's Institute for Social Research between the world wars. Questions stemming from Marxist thought, such as the acute crises of capitalism and the persistence of authoritarianism, preoccupied its loosely affiliated members. Including Max Horkheimer, Theodore Adorno (author of *The Authoritarian Personality*, discussed in Chapter 2), Herbert Marcuse, and others (Held, 1980), they were critical not only of political systems but also of science and knowledge itself. Originally focused on Europe, the Frankfurt School gained influence in the United States against a backdrop of sweeping social change and a general distrust of authority during the 1960s. Political economy's focus on the interconnections between politics and economics aligned with the critical perspective's major questions, and the critical perspective imparted an enduring interest in class struggle and imbalances of power. The resulting scholarship on political economy paid careful attention to how institutions such as capitalism and the state marginalized social groups based on categories such as gender, social class, and race and ethnicity (Estes, Linkens, & Binney, 2001). Hence, in its revived form, political economy was first and foremost a perspective critical of existing power dynamics, ideology, and inequality.

The Political Economy of Aging: A Conceptual Model

Beginning in the late 1970s, gerontologists have extended political economy to the issues and problems surrounding aging (Estes et al., 2001). Notably, Estes (2001) has presented a conceptual model of the political economy of aging (shown in Figure 8.1) that specifically outlines ways in which individuals and groups can use ideologies to support their policy agendas. In Estes' (2001) model, the state, financial and post-industrial capital, the sex-gender system, the citizen/public, and the aging enterprise create and sustain policies relate to aging. We use her model to structure this chapter because of its explicit focus on the interconnections between public policy (the state) and other aspects of power and inequality, and because of its attention to ideologies such as ageisms.

The Uses of Ideology

Within the framework of political economy, ideologies include broad perspectives such as liberalism and conservatism and more focused systems of thought such as compassionate ageism and generational equity. In the United States, compassionate ageism, which stereotypes the elderly as poor, frail, and deserving of aid (Binstock, 2010), remains the dominant ideology of old age in policy, but its influence on some policy areas has eroded over time. In part, this erosion has occurred due to demographic and economic changes, but has also depended on how successfully individuals and groups have used alternative ideologies.

Estes (2001) details three processes through which ideologies help to support and sustain social policy. First, ideologies allow experts, the media, policy makers, and others to create cultural images that support their political and economic agendas. For instance, the generational equity frame, which includes the idea that the elderly are taking more than their fair share of

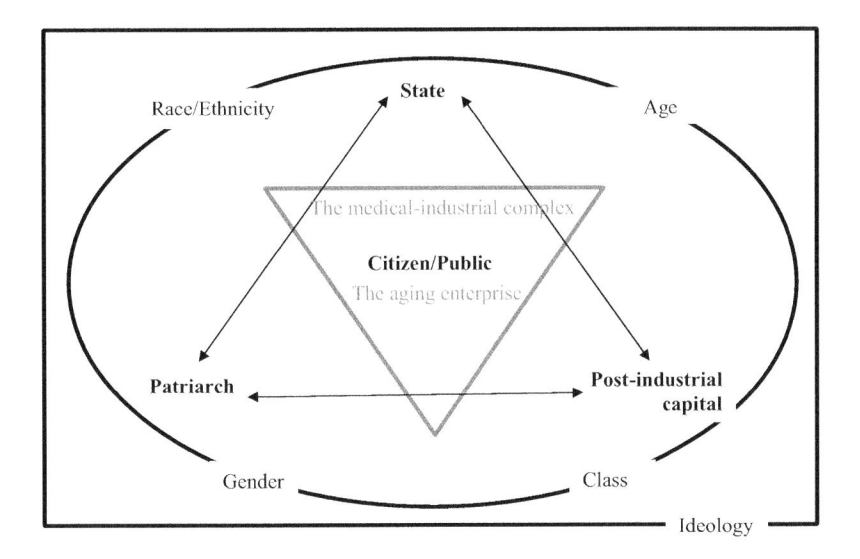

Figure 8.1 Theoretical model of social policy and aging
Source: adapted from Estes, 2001

resources at the expense of the young, serves as the source material for cultural images of "greedy geezers." Second, ideologies help elites formulate appeals to the economic system. For example, an ideology that puts the blame for the state's fiscal crises on the elderly, the poor, or other social groups provides a logic for cutting back on social welfare programs that may be acceptable to the public because it appeals to ideas of fairness. Third, ideologies provide ways to implement systems that appear outwardly rational or technical, but actually disguise inequalities and defuse conflict-laden situations. A policy that makes women reliant on men for their income in old age, for instance, might provoke outrage. But while Social Security is technically gender-neutral, women rely on their spouses' earnings history for their benefits more often than men do. The system then disguises these built-in gender inequalities.

Connections with Public Policy

Estes' (2001) model draws attention to the relationships between the state and other systems, including financial and post-industrial capital, the sex/gender system, the citizen/public, and the aging enterprise. She defines the **state** broadly, including the branches of government, the military, the criminal justice system, and public health, welfare, and educational institutions. In this chapter, we consider the state primarily in relation to public policy. **Financial and post-industrial capital** refers to corporations, their assets, and their methods of pursuing their interests in a globalized economy. Estes (2001) emphasizes that the globalization of capital has supported a number of other processes, including privatization, rationalization, deregulation, and competition. The **sex/gender system** includes the way in which gendered institutions, such as the state and families, transform biological sexuality into human activities. Under the influence of feminist theory, political economy has looked at the diverse ways in which the sex/gender system subordinates women. At the intersection of the state, capital, and the sex/gender system, the **citizen/public** refers to the benefits and rights of citizens. Rather than considering all citizenship equal, political economy emphasizes that citizenship is unequally distributed (Estes, 2001). Some people have more power, more money, and more influence than others.

The **aging enterprise**, located at the intersection of the state, the sex/gender system, and post-industrial capital, refers to the "programs, organizations, bureaucracies, interest groups, trade associations, providers, industries, and professionals that serve the aged in one capacity or another" (Estes, 1979, p. 2). The **medical-industrial complex** is a subset of the aging enterprise that focuses on medical services for the elderly. Both treat the elderly's care (or the elderly's health care, in the case of the medical-industrial complex) as commodities, economic products to be bought and sold, rather than as social goods. Within this framework, organizations aim to maximize profits (Estes, 2001). While some individuals and organizations might seek to provide the best service possible for the elderly, there is constant pressure to prioritize on the bottom line. We spend less time in this chapter discussing the aging enterprise and medical-industrial complex than the other levels, in part because much of this material is covered in Chapter 7.

Ageism and Public Policy: Three Policies, Three Uses for Ideology

In this chapter, we discuss the three uses of ideology that Estes details in the context of aging policy. Further, we argue that these ideologies have had a long reach in shaping the connections between public policy (the state) and financial and post-industrial capital, the sex/gender system, and the citizen/public. To illustrate the three uses of ideology, we use three very different arenas of public policy: elder abuse policy, the Age Discrimination in Employment Act, and public pensions.

Elder Abuse Policies: The Creation of Cultural Images

An irresponsible teenager. A querulous old man. A frail old woman. You can probably picture each of these **cultural images**, representations of cultural beliefs, without difficulty. But how do certain cultural images become enshrined in our imaginations, while others do not? Estes (2001) argues that individuals and groups use ideologies as sources of these images. If successful, the images serve as fuel to support certain policy agendas. For example, as a policy issue the emergence of **elder abuse**—a caregiver's intentional actions to cause harm or risk of harm to a vulnerable elder, or a caregiver's failure to satisfy the elder's basic needs (Lachs & Pillemer, 2004)—has depended in part on the use of cultural images.

A Cultural Image: The Battered Granny

In the 1970s, a stream of articles (Baker, 1975; Burston, 1975) appeared on "granny-battering" or "granny-bashing." Drawing on the ideology of compassionate ageism, the scholarly and media attention conjured up a frail old woman, a person who could not possibly stand up to physical abuse at the hands of relatives at home or of staff in institutions. An article in the British newspaper the *Guardian* exemplified this cultural image, declaring that "Old people can be bruised simply by being led firmly across a busy street. Their bones are fragile and they are often a little unsteady on their feet; an angry shove is enough to send them sprawling on to the floor" (Renvoize, 1976, p. 9).

The United States adopted legislation to protect the elderly from abuse against the backdrop of this cultural image. Today, most policies that aim to prevent elder abuse are elements of larger laws, including: the Older Americans Act, which funds support state- and local-level programs; the Violence against Women Act, which provides some grants focused on older women; and the Elder Justice Act, which focuses on demonstration programs, training, and services related to elder abuse (Dong & Simon, 2011). In light of the importance of the cultural image of the battered granny, it is not surprising that the underlying logic of the elder care abuse system in the United States aligns closely with compassionate ageism. Adult protective services programs mirror child protective services programs, as both function under a model of *parens patriae*, in which the state provides protection for citizens unable to protect themselves (Brownell, 2010). *Parens patriae* assumes that older adults are unable or unwilling to make appropriate decisions for themselves, much like children. This may be true of some older adults, such as those with advanced dementia (Arias, 2013), but the protection-oriented approach of the elder abuse system extends in subtle ways to older adults who are competent to make their own decisions.

Connections: A Protection-Oriented Approach

There are two primary ways in which elder abuse law intersects with financial and post-industrial capital, and its protection-oriented slant colors both. First, some elder abuse occurs in nursing homes and other institutions, what Estes (2001) terms the medical-industrial complex. While prosecutors may bring cases against nursing home chains under a diverse range of statutes, such as the False Claims Act (Connolly, 2010), institutions can also face potential charges under the protection-oriented model of elder abuse. Second, some business interests aim to curb elder abuse, but to be eligible for government funding they often focus on protection or rehabilitation of the elderly, rather than on their empowerment. For example, one New York service agency that focused on empowering female victims of elder abuse was not eligible for reimbursement from government funding sources because it did not fit into rehabilitative services (Brownell, 2010). Hence, the long-term slant toward the protection rather than empowerment of the elderly continues to have implications for corporations.

Another reason for the protection-oriented slant of elder abuse policies is historical. Medical professionals have been largely responsible for identifying elder abuse. The treatment, protection, and rehabilitation of elderly victims are common concerns. Over the same period, the women's movement has identified abuse of younger women as an important issue. In line with feminism and the women's movement, hearing and empowering victims have become hallmarks of programs to stem the abuse of women. The historical division of key stakeholders means that "elder abuse" and "battered women" remain distinct problems, with distinct approaches (Hightower, 2010).

Further, within the protection-oriented framework of elder abuse policy, not all potential victims receive the same attention. In part because a disproportionate number of victims are women (Roberto, 2016), elder abuse of men has become an invisible problem (Kosberg, 2010). Further, the terminology of "elder abuse" masks wide discrepancies in experience by age. Adults age 75 and older are more likely than those aged 60 to 69 to experience financial abuse, while the "young old" (aged 60 to 69) are more likely to experience other forms of abuse because they are more likely to live with a spouse or adult children (Roberto, 2016). Many of these victims do not fit the image of the "battered granny" or the protection-oriented approach of elder abuse policy neatly, making their abuse more difficult to understand and combat within the existing ideology.

Appeals to the Economic System: The Age Discrimination in Employment Act

Consider the following statement: "Forcing older workers to retire before they want to do so wastes experienced labor." This logic for allowing older workers to remain in the labor force, while it might work to their advantage, is an appeal to the economic system rather than to their rights as human beings or to the concepts of fairness or justice. Such appeals have provided counter arguments to **succession ageism**, the set of cultural beliefs and assumptions about the proper time for older adults to make way for the younger generation (North & Fiske, 2013), and have aided in the establishment of the **Age Discrimination in Employment Act (ADEA).**

The Bottom Line: A "Loss to a Nation on the Move"

Prior to the abolishment of mandatory retirement, succession ageism meant that there was a socially correct time for older workers to step aside and give younger workers a chance to move up the career ladder. But mandatory retirement made business sense as well. As economist Edward Lazear (1979) noted, employers used these policies to control costs. To keep workers motivated, they paid younger workers less than their work was worth, and older workers more than their work was worth. But this system was too expensive if older workers remained on the job beyond a certain age. Mandatory retirement, under the auspices of succession ageism, helped to keep these costs down in a way that many people considered fair or right.

The definition of mandatory retirement as a "problem" depended on an appeal to the economic system. An improved economy in the 1950s and 1960s drew attention to the problem of workers forced to retire (Macnicol, 2006). As President Johnson said in 1967,

> There are thousands of retired teachers, lawyers, businessmen, social workers and recreation specialists, physicians, nurses, and others, who possess skills which the country badly needs. Hundreds of thousands… find themselves jobless because of arbitrary age discrimination… In economic terms, this is a serious—and senseless—loss to a nation on the move.
>
> (Johnson, 1967)

Johnson (1967) went on to say that the greater loss was to the happiness of the older workers and their families, but the appeal to the economic system remained strong in the push to end mandatory retirement. The 1967 ADEA was partly a response to these concerns. It prevented private-sector employers with 25 of more employees from discriminating against workers aged 45 to 65 on the basis of age (Macnicol, 2006). Over the next 20 years, the ADEA's scope and coverage gradually expanded, including local, state, and federal employees; reducing the minimum company size; increasing the protected age range from 40 to 70; and eventually eliminating the upper age limit. This last change, in 1986, effectively outlawed mandatory retirement for most Americans (Neumark, 2003).

Connections: The Title VII-ADEA Gap

The ways in which courts have addressed age discrimination claims under the ADEA have favored business interests in various ways. We argue that appeals to the economic system have remained a prominent aspect of court rulings, resulting in a number of critical gaps between Title VII of the Civil Rights Act (which forbids employment discrimination based on sex, race, color, national origin, and religion) and the ADEA. As one court put it, "neither Congress nor the state Legislature ever intended the age discrimination laws to inhibit the very process by which a free market economy—decision making on the basis of cost—is conducted and by which, ultimately, real jobs and wealth are created" (Marks v. Loral Corp., 1997).

From the perspective of financial and post-industrial capital, it is difficult for employees to bring successful suit under the ADEA as compared to Title VII (Harper, 2012). In Title VII cases, employers may make employment decisions that disproportionately affect people in protected classes if they can prove it is a business necessity. For instance, women may be adversely affected by physical fitness testing for firefighting positions, but the employer can use the fitness tests if they accurately measure effective job performance and that performance is necessary to accomplish the job safely and effectively. The ADEA differs in that employers do not need to prove that an action adversely affecting older workers is a "business necessity." They can use a **reasonable factor other than age (RFOA)** defense, arguing only that the decision was "reasonable" (Rothenberg & Gardner, 2011).

Further, the Civil Rights Act allows for a limited mixed-motive theory, which can entitle a plaintiff to an order requiring employers to stop using that factor (such as gender) in its decisions, plus court costs and attorney fees, if they can show that that factor played *any* role in the employer's decision. But according to a 2009 Supreme Court Case, the same is not true of the ADEA. In that case, *Gross* v. *FBL Financial Services Inc.* (2009), a company demoted a 54-year-old worker as part of a corporate restructuring. The Supreme Court held that the plaintiff needed to prove that age was the "but for" cause of the employment action, meaning that "but for" the plaintiff's age the company would not have demoted him (Farnum & Wiener, 2016).

The ADEA also allows employers to consider age in employment decisions if it is a **bona fide occupational qualification (BFOQ)**, meaning that a worker over a certain age could not perform the job adequately. The situations in which age might be considered a BFOQ, including a variety of public-safety occupations such as firefighters and airline pilots (Rothenberg & Gardner, 2011), are broader than those for which gender could be considered a BFOQ.

There is also a daunting barrier to bringing suit against a corporation based on systemic ageism. Imagine a job posting stating that the ideal candidate would be a "digital native." Because of the widespread perception that younger workers are more technology-savvy, this might lay the groundwork for age discrimination in hiring. But putting together a class action lawsuit of older workers who applied unsuccessfully for these jobs would be difficult because, under ADEA procedures, each potential plaintiff would need to "opt in," or consent in writing to being included in the case. Title VII, in direct contrast, allows class action lawsuits to use an opt-out procedure. All women would be part of a gender discrimination lawsuit unless they opted out (Harper, 2012). The ADEA's opt-in procedure for class action lawsuits makes it difficult for plaintiffs to build a case against systemic age discrimination.

A further difficulty in age-discrimination claims arises from the connection between the state and the sex/gender system. Title VII allows for "sex plus" discrimination cases, in which the plaintiffs argue that a subset of a protected class has been the victim of discrimination (Porter, 2003). For instance, in Phillips v. Martin Marietta Corp. (1971), the defendant had a policy of not hiring women with pre-school-aged children. The Supreme Court held that, even though their hiring policy did not affect all women, having different hiring policies for men and women was discriminatory. In a similar case, Sprogis v. United Air Lines (1971), an airline required its female flight attendants to be unmarried while men could be married or unmarried. The Seventh Circuit court ruled that, although the policy affected only some women, it was still discriminatory. In Jeffries v. Harris County Community Action Association (1980), the employer passed a black woman over for promotion and later fired her. The Fifth Circuit court held that it was possible for practices to discriminate against black women, even if they did not discriminate against white women or black men (Porter, 2003). Each of these cases established that "sex plus" other characteristics could be grounds for discrimination. But, with some exceptions (such as Arnett v. Aspin, 1994), comparatively few courts have addressed "sex plus age" discrimination (Porter, 2003). Most courts treat sex- and age-discrimination claims separately, under the theory that sex-discrimination claims fall under Title VII while age-discrimination claims fall under the ADEA (Day, 2014).

While the ADEA aims to stem age discrimination, it does not protect all citizens equally. The ADEA protects only workers aged 40 and older, and even within the protected class does not allow for reverse discrimination claims. A 2004 Supreme Court case, *General Dynamics Land Systems, Inc. v. Cline*, concerned reverse age discrimination under the ADEA. The General Dynamics Land Systems company, as the result of collective bargaining, eliminated retiree health benefits for employees who had not reached 50 years of age or 30 years of job tenure by 1997. A group of employees aged 40 to 49 reasoned that they had been the victims of reverse age discrimination, and because they were within the protected age range for the ADEA, they believed that the statute should protect them. In direct contrast to rulings that allowed for reverse discrimination claims under Title VII, the Supreme Court majority emphasized that the ADEA was designed to protect older workers from discrimination in favor of younger workers, not the reverse (Green, 2004). Consequently, compared to Title VII, the ADEA not only covers fewer workers (those aged 40 and up), it does not cover reverse discrimination within that age range.

Public Pension Programs: Policies as Rational Problem Solving

Estes (2001) argues that one of the uses of ideology is "the implementation of policy and the application of expertise in ways that transform conflicts over goals and means into systems of rational problem solving." That is, ideologies allow us to address conflict-laden situations in ways that seem rational, but which often obscure conflict and inequalities based on race, ethnicity, gender, social class, and age. Perhaps in no arena of public policy is this process more evident than in **public pension** systems, systems such as Social Security which aim to provide financial support in old age. They also provide one of the clearest examples of how ideologies such as compassionate ageism provide the support to implement systems of rational problem solving.

Rational Problem Solving: The Structure of Pension Plans

Ideologies such as compassionate ageism serve as the source material to establish that the elderly deserve financial support, but the way in which that source material is transformed into pension systems differs substantially across nations. One of the primary ways in which the structure of public pension plans differs is the degree to which they redistribute wealth within generations. In **Bismarkian pension plans**, a person's benefits depend on their individual earning history, so there is little redistribution of wealth among older adults. **Beveridgean pension plans** instead give lower-income individuals higher rates of return on their earnings, focusing on providing the elderly with an adequate basic income and effectively redistributing wealth from higher earners to lower earners (Rivera-Roso, García-Huitrón, Steenbeek, & van der Lecq, 2018). As shown in Figure 8.2, most pension plans fall somewhere between these two extremes. Tim Krieger and Stefan Traub's (2013) **Bismarkian Factor**, a measure of how Bismarkian or Beveridgean a public pension program is, indicates that Denmark and Australia are almost entirely Beveridgean with scores close to 0. The United States is close to 0.50 with prominent Bismarkian and Beveridgean elements. The mechanisms of Bismarkian and Beveridgean systems obscure the class dynamics of old-age support. Rather than explicitly focusing on social class, they provide a rational-seeming system of rules linking income during working years to income in later life.

Connections: Complex Systems from Ideology

The Bismarkian or Beveridgean tilt of public pensions is of critical importance to financial capital. In many countries public pensions represent a large proportion of the total assets under financial management. Additionally, because Beveridgean systems provide a flat benefit, they make private pensions attractive and typically necessary for maintaining adequate financial resources in later life (Aggarwal & Goodell, 2013).

Adding to the complexity of pension schemes, most public pension plans pay **derived benefits**, or benefits based on the work histories of a related person, such as a spouse or parent, to older adults with limited work histories (Leroux & Pestieau, 2011). For those who have spent much of their lives as homemakers, the rules of the pension programs tie derived benefits

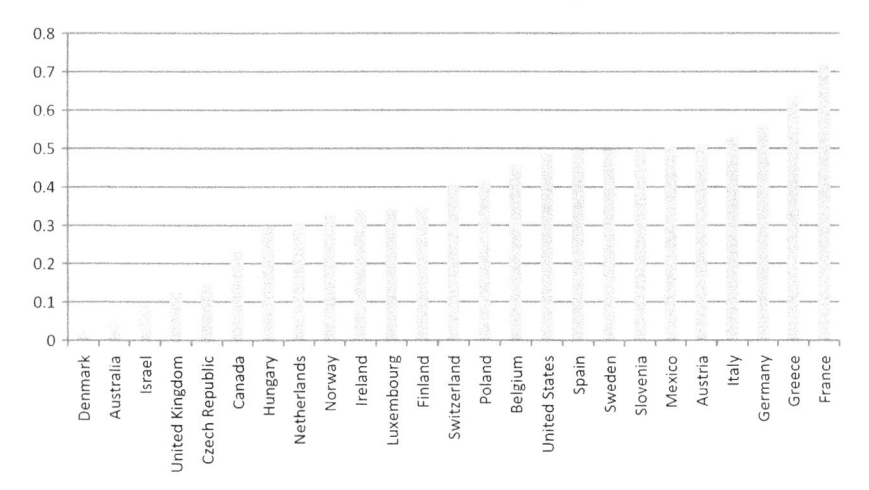

Figure 8.2 Bismarkian factors
Note: data averaged for Czechoslovakia (1988–92) and the Czech Republic (1993–7 and 2003–4). Data averaged for Slovenia (1992–2004). For all other countries, data averaged 1988 to 2008
Source: Rivera-Roso et al., 2018

to the wages of their spouse or former spouse. Because women earn less than men and spend more time out of the labor force, they are more likely to receive pension benefits based on derived rights, and because benefits from derived rights are typically lower than benefits from a person's own work history, they tend to be less well-off financially in retirement. Accordingly, the **replacement rate**, or the percentage of the workers' income that their public pension benefits replaces, is lowest among women. For instance, one 2006 study of Organisation for Economic Co-operation and Development countries found that non-working widows averaged a replacement rate of 36 percent, compared to 50 percent for working widows and almost 60 percent for married couples (Choi, 2006). Derived rights are generally beneficial to women but they have a deep connection with the sex-gender system, as they are one of the main ways in which older women are financially dependent on the state.

Similar to derived rights, the **earnings test** translated the ideology of compassionate ageism into a complex system of rational problem solving. Compassionate ageism meant that the elderly should receive benefits if they could not work. But once a person earned over a low exempt amount, the earnings test reduced their Social Security benefits in proportion to any additional earnings. The calculations led to higher benefits later in exchange for these reductions, but most people perceived the earnings test as a direct loss of income. Beginning in the 1970s, a series of changes increased the exempt amount and eliminated the earnings test for certain age groups (Friedberg, 2000). The 2000 Senior Citizens Freedom to Work Act removed the earnings test for workers at or past the **normal retirement age**, the age at which people could claim full Social Security benefits (Song & Manchester, 2007). Today, the earnings test only affects workers younger than the normal retirement age (Social Security Administration, n.d.).

Public pension policy transforms ideology into systems of rational problem solving in complex ways. These systems often obscure inequalities based on sex, race, ethnicity, social class, and age. For instance, Beveridgean elements of public pension plans direct financial resources to lower-income individuals. Derived rights provide financial support for women, many of whom have spent less time in the labor force than men. The earnings test, to the extent that it still applies, directs immediate benefits away from higher-earning individuals. Hence, the programs draw their original support from ideologies such as compassionate ageism, but the systems obscure some of the more blatant inequalities in old age.

Ideological Arguments for Age-Restricted Communities: From Compassionate Ageism

At the beginning of this chapter, we asked why we so readily accept age discrimination in housing. Below, we make an argument for age-restricted communities that uses ideology in the three ways that Estes (2001) details. Each of these arguments draws on compassionate ageism, but uses this cultural reservoir of ideas in different ways. One argument appeals to cultural images of the lonely widow:

> Imagine a lonely old widow. Because she is frail, she is not able to drive long distances to visit friends anymore. She spends her days physically isolated, because most of her neighbors are families in which all adults work. An age-restricted community is appropriate for her, because there will be more people around to socialize with during the day, and because activities are available on the grounds.

This "lonely old widow" cultural image draws directly on compassionate ageism. From this perspective, age-restricted communities are appropriate because they cater to a population that deserves special treatment. A second argument makes an appeal to the economic system:

> The elderly deserve communities in which they can be as independent as possible, but most American communities do not have the resources to make life really comfortable for them. It would be expensive to rebuild public buildings to be one floor, for instance. From this perspective, age-restricted communities designed specifically for the elderly make good financial sense.

This appeal to the economic system relies on compassionate ageism, in that it hinges on the deservingness and financial limitations of the elderly. However, it also appeals directly to the cost of making communities accessible to the elderly. A third argument rests on a system of rational problem solving:

> A substantial number of older adults want to downsize their homes after their children have grown up to reduce their costs. Their lower retirement income means that many detached homes might be outside of their budgets. Age-restricted communities help to address this problem because they offer small, often one bedroom, detached homes at affordable prices.

Like the other arguments for age-restricted communities, this argument draws indirectly on compassionate ageism by highlighting the comparative economic neediness of the elderly. But it differs from the other arguments in that it emphasizes the "problem-solving" aspect of the policy.

Conclusion

In this chapter, we used political economy as a lens to examine the role of ideology in public policy. We looked at three areas of public policy, corresponding to uses of ideology: as a source of cultural images, as an appeal to the economic system, and as an aspect of systems of rational problem solving. While we used three areas of policy as examples of each of these three uses of ideology, in reality individuals and groups are likely to use ideology in more than one of these ways when promoting a policy. Hence, in the final section of this chapter, we used compassionate ageism to support age-restricted communities in three ways.

Discussion Questions

1. In this chapter, we used the ideology of compassionate ageism to support age-restricted communities in three ways. Can you think of arguments *against* age-restricted communities using (a) a cultural image, (b) an appeal to the economic system, and (c) a system of rational problem solving? If so, what ideologies (e.g., generational equity) would you draw on to make these arguments?
2. Consider the question of succession ageism. Do you think there is a "right" age for older workers to step aside to give younger workers a chance at desirable jobs and promotions? Why or why not?
3. In the Introduction, we presented an argument for age-restricted communities based on the idea of age as lifestyle. In this chapter, we instead presented an argument based on compassionate ageism. Which logic do you find more convincing? Why?

Conclusion

The Ghosts of Ageism's Future: Five Take-Away Messages

Is ageism the elephant or the mouse? At the start of this book, we argued that ageism is more often the mouse. We have spent the majority of this book putting ageism in perspective (Chapters 1 through 4, Part I) and in context (Chapters 5 through 8, Part II), and throughout we have looked at both the past of ageism and its present. But, we have spent little time considering the future of ageism. In this chapter, we bring together the materials from Parts I and II to discuss five take-away messages from this book related to ageism—past and present—and their potential implications for the future.

These are: (1) ageism is about better or worse, not yes or no; (2) we're all winners and losers. But mostly losers; (3) it's all about the frame (or the ideology); (4) we need to start talking about "ageism plus"; and (5) there is more than one path forward for institutional ageism. While drawn from earlier material in this book, the five take-away messages stand on their own as examples of potential pathways for the future of ageism.

Take-Away 1: Ageism Is about Better or Worse, Not Yes or No

Can we beat ageism? Like most social problems, it is not amenable to a simple solution. In an influential 1973 article on planning, Horst Rittel and Melvin Webber write that societal problems differ inherently from the problems of the natural sciences. Many, including ageism, are **wicked problems**, ill-defined and difficult to address. Rittel and Webber (1973) identify ten criteria to define wicked problems, two of which are particularly relevant to this take-away message. First, they argue that "Wicked problems have no stopping rule" (p. 162). Because we never fully and finally solve wicked problems, there is no point at which we can "stop" attempting to solve them. If we choose not to work on ageism as a social problem, it is because of a lack of political buy-in or interest, not because we can ever fully and finally solve the problem. Second, they state that "There is no immediate and no ultimate test of a solution to a wicked problem" (p. 163). Any social change will have a host of unintended consequences over a long period of time. For example, a public awareness campaign against compassionate ageism could unintentionally erode support for programs such as Social Security, causing financial distress among older adults. Hence, we argue that we may never eradicate ageism, but we can reduce ageism and improve conditions related to age discrimination.

Take-Away 2: We're All Winners and Losers. But Mostly Losers

Should we want to beat ageism? One of the key defining characteristics of ageism is that it is prejudice directed toward our future (or former) selves. Consequently, any type of ageism from which we benefit at one point in our lives, we will suffer at another point. We will all experience ageism directed at our age group at one point in time; in fact, the development of ageism segments in different media, discussed in Chapter 5, means that we may experience positive ageism from some media sources, such as specific magazines, and negative ageism from other media sources, such as youth culture, at the same time. And, in some contexts such as the workplace, both the old and young can be the targets of discrimination and prejudice at the same time, as we discussed in Chapter 7. Overall, ageism is both good and bad for individuals, but its deleterious effects over the life course are likely to override any benefits while we are in the favored groups.

Take-Away 3: It's All about the Frame (or the Ideology)

What is a critical hidden aspect of ageism? In Chapter 3, we discussed how frames, as organizers of everyday experience, draw our attention to real-world evidence, suggest what the real issues and questions are, and help to define what we should do about and for social issues. We further develop this concept in the context of political economy's ideologies in Chapter 8, adopting Caroll Estes' (2001) model of the political economy of aging. She argues that ideologies allow individuals and groups to create cultural images to support their agendas, help them to formulate appeals to the economic system, and allow them to implement systems that appear outwardly rational or technical. Some frames, such as the ideal worker and ideal career frame, which we discuss in Chapter 7, are context-specific. The ideal worker frame organizes our experience of the workplace around an "ideal worker" who has few if any family responsibilities and puts in long hours at work. The ideal career frame organizes our experience around an "ideal career" with an early part during which a person establishes themselves and "learns the ropes," a middle part during which they are most productive and established, and an end part where they disengage from the labor force. A key aspect of ageism is framing or ideology, and by extension the future of ageism depends largely on what frames or ideologies prevail.

Take-Away 4: We Need to Start Talking about "Ageism Plus"

How should we talk about ageism? In Chapter 8, we discussed how the ADEA does not allow for "age plus" claims easily, while Title VII allows for "sex plus" claims. In other chapters, we have provided ample evidence that we need to start talking about "age plus" and even "ageism plus." In Chapter 4, we discussed the role of intersectionality, the interconnections between the experiences and perceptions of social categories such as age, race, and gender. Research such as Kang and Chasteen's (2009) facing study highlights the complexity of these interconnections. They found that, for older black men, the likeable elderly man stereotype eclipsed the hostile black male stereotype. In Chapter 7, we discussed other manifestations of intersectionality. For instance, Neumark et al. (2016)'s study of fictional job applicants found substantially more age discrimination in call-backs for women than for men. We argue that the future of ageism is more about "ageism plus" other forms of prejudice such as racism and sexism than about "ageism alone."

Take-Away 5: There Is More than One Path Forward for Institutional Ageism

The future of ageism depends partly on what variations of ageisms become institutionalized through social policies. To date, the dominant form of institutional ageism has been **structured dependence**. The term, which sociologist Peter Townsend (1981) coined, refers to ways in which social policies marginalize older adults and render them economically dependent on the state. We argue here that there are two other potential paths forward for institutional ageism: structured dependence, structured independence, and structured interdependence. First, **structured independence** is a potential form of institutional ageism that maps on to the generational equity frame, which we have discussed in more detail in Chapter 4. The advocates of this frame focused on cuts to existing programs, beginning with Social Security and Medicare spending and later spilled over to diverse programs including subsidized housing (Williamson & Rhodes, 2011). Ultimately, the enactment of such cuts would have ushered in an era of structured independence, in which the elderly primarily relied on their own savings and assets for support. Second, **structured interdependence** is a potential form of institutional ageism growing out of the literature on productive aging. For a number of years, most people considered physical and mental decline a part of "normal aging." Rather than focusing on age-related declines, the concept of **productive aging** focused on the continued activities of older adults, such as paid and unpaid work, helping others, and caregiving (Johnson & Mutchler, 2013). Advocates of productive aging, such as gerontologist Nancy Morrow-Howell, have offered concrete policies using productive aging as an ideology of old age. In a recent letter to the president-elect and congress, she and her colleagues suggest three types of policies. These include: policies that encourage longer working lives, such as by increasing tax incentives for adopting flexible work arrangements attractive to older workers; providing social and financial support to caregivers, such as by allowing family caregiving time to count toward a worker's employment history for the purposes of Social Security; and promoting federal support for older volunteers, such as expanding and funding organizations such as the Corporation for National and Community Services (Morrow-Howell, Gonzales, Harootyan, Lee, & Lindberg, 2017). Hence, structured independence and interdependence offer two alternative pathways for institutional ageism, each with their own policy implications.

Conclusion

In this chapter, we propose five take-away messages, based on the earlier material in this book. We argue that: (1) ageism is about better or worse, not yes or no; (2) we're all winners and losers. But mostly losers; (3) it's all about the frame (or the ideology); (4) we need to start talking about "ageism plus"; and (5) there is more than one path forward for institutional ageism. While drawn primarily from what we know about the past and present of ageism, they also have implications for its future.

Discussion Questions

1 We have proposed five take-away messages for the future of ageism. Based on other material from this book, what additional messages would you propose?
2 There are a number of paths forward for institutional ageism, including structured dependence, structured independence, and structured interdependence. Consider one of these pathways and discuss what you see as its advantages and disadvantages for older adults and society.

Glossary

acute medicalization   The process of defining and treating a problem as an acute medical condition
age discrimination   Unfair or unequal treatment targeting older people
Age Discrimination in Employment Act (ADEA)   Federal law prohibiting age discrimination against most workers age 40 and older
age-as-leveler hypothesis   Hypothesis stating that inequalities tend to decrease with age
ageism   Stereotypes or prejudices based on age
ageism segments   Stereotype segments referring to older adults
age-restricted housing communities   Communities that restrict ownership or renting based on age
aging enterprise   In political economy, the organizations and groups that serve the aged
anti-ageist   Stereotypes that promote growing older without the negative aspects of aging
audit studies   Studies in which fictional interviewees are coached to act identically but have different demographic characteristics
authoritarian personality   An abnormally fascist and prejudiced personality that developed due to overly strict childhoods; from a psychoanalytic theory
authority shift   Shift from traditional values to secular-rational values, predicted by the value modernization framework
Beveridgean pension plan   A type of pension plan which gives lower-income individuals higher rates of return on their earnings as compared to higher-income individuals
Bismarkian factor   Tim Krieger and Stefan Traub's (2013) measure of how Bismarkian or Beveridgean a public pension program is
Bismarkian pension plan   A type of pension plan in which a person's benefits depend on their individual earning history
bona fide occupational qualification (BFOQ)   Defense which, under the ADEA, allows employers to take age into account if workers over a certain age could not perform the job

career development theory A human resource management theory that defines a career as a series of successive developmental tasks

chronosystem The changes over time in the micro, meso, exo, and macrosystems

citizen/public In political economy, the benefits and rights of citizens

collective frame break Collective experiences that "break frame." *See* frame break

communication accommodation theory A framework for understanding how people use communication to accentuate, reduce, or maintain social distance

comorbidity The presence of two or more diseases or conditions

confirmers Individuals who appear to fit the group stereotype

content analysis Systematic analysis of the content of media

convergence theory A theory that predicts that the economic and social conditions prevalent in developed economies cause different societies to become more similar structurally and culturally over time

correspondence studies Studies in which fictional resumes are identical in terms of qualifications but differ in easily discernible demographic characteristics

cultivation theory Macro-level theory explaining how media cultivate assumptions about the world

cultural images Representations of cultural beliefs

culture The knowledge and characteristics of society in general

cumulative inequality Theoretical perspective that focuses on how inequality accumulates over time

developmental psychology The study of human change over the life span

disconfirmers Individuals who appear not to fit the group stereotype

disparate impact Legal doctrine that states that a policy can be discriminatory if it has an adverse impact against a group

divergence A communication strategy which accentuates the verbal and non-verbal differences between the speaker and their audience

double jeopardy (multiple jeopardy) Combined effects of multiple oppressive barriers, including not only racism and sexism but also discrimination based on class or sexuality

earnings test A policy that reduced a person's Social Security benefits by an amount proportional to their earnings from pay

ecological model A model of how human development occurs in the context of a number of fields or "systems" surrounding the individual

economic development A broad term for the stage, state, or level of an economy as it relates to the well-being of the people living within it

efficacy expectations In social learning theory, the beliefs that a person can execute a behavior

elder abuse A caregiver's intentional actions to cause harm to or fail to satisfy the basic needs of a vulnerable elder

elderspeak The patronizing talk directed toward the elderly

exosystem A linkage between two or more settings, one of which the individual participates in and one of which they do not participate in

fair innings ageism Ageism which gives priority to the young because of the belief that they have not yet had a fair chance at life

filial responsibility law Placed financial responsibility for supporting impoverished older adults on relatives, typically their adult children

financial and post-industrial capital In political economy, corporations, their assets and their methods of pursuing their interests in a globalized economy

frame A set of rules and premises that provide meaning to everyday experience

frame analysis a research method that focuses on the frames that give meaning to everyday experience

frame break The act of stepping outside of the rules and expectations of a frame

Frankfurt School School of philosophical and social thought that originated at Frankfurt's Institute for Social Research between the world wars

generational accounting Method of evaluating the fiscal impact of policies by calculating a lifetime net tax rate; related to the generational equity

generational equity debate A debate, originating in the 1980s between two competing frames for understanding the elderly, generational interdependence, and generational equity frames

generational equity frame Frame which emphasized the extent to which the elderly might be getting more than their fair share at the expense of children and younger adults

generational interdependence frame Frame which emphasized the ways in which generations and age cohorts are interdependent rather than competing or conflicting

great risk shift Systematic transfer of economic risk from large organizations and government to individuals and families

homo liberalismus Esping-Andersen's term for the American ideal, combines self-reliance with voluntary altruism; dominant frame for understanding ageism until the mid-1980s

ideal career frame A frame that defines and organizes work around a typical career at which mid-career workers are at their highest performance

ideal worker frame A frame that defines and organizes work around a typically male worker with few to no family responsibilities

ideologies Systems of ideas. *See also* frame

individual frame break Individual acts that "break frame." *See* frame break

industrialization The transition from agricultural and commercial economies to industrial economies

in-group The group of which the individual considers him or herself a member

in-group favoritism Preferential perceptions or treatment of members of the in-group

institutional ageism Unfair or unequal treatment based on age embedded in institutions

intersectionality Interconnections between perceptions and experiences of different social categories, such as race and ethnicity, gender, age, and sexual orientation

law against miserliness A problem-solving approach that calls for avoiding an explanation that is too simple to fit the evidence

life course perspective Theoretical perspective that focuses on how the life course, the sequence of events and roles that individuals enact over the course of their lives, is embedded in social, historical, geographic, and other contexts

lifetime net tax rate What a social group, usually a generation, would pay in taxes minus the government transfers that they could expect to receive under various assumptions; a key concept in generational accounting

macro level Dealing primarily with large groups or society as a whole

macrosystem The overarching pattern of systems that characterize a culture

maintenance A communication strategy which adheres to the original communication style regardless of the audience

market segmentation The division of consumers based on their characteristics and the products they would be most likely to buy

mass education A system of compulsory national education

Matthew Effect Term for process by which advantage accumulates. *See also* cumulative inequality

media studies The academic study of mass media

medical-industrial complex In political economy, the organizations and groups that provide health care to the aged. A subset of the aging enterprise

medicalization The process of defining and treating a problem in medical terms

mesosystem A linkage between two or more settings in which the individual participates

micro level Dealing primarily with individuals and small groups

microsystem The activities, roles, and relationships that occur in face-to-face settings

models In social learning theory, individuals to observe and imitate

modernization The shift from agricultural to industrial modes of production, together with accompanying social and cultural changes

modernization theory A theory of historical development that posits, among other social and cultural changes, declining status of the aged

mortality salience hypothesis A hypothesis that when people are more aware of their own mortality, they adhere more strongly to cultural values. *See also* terror management theory

near out-groups (near in-groups) Groups that we view more favorably than true out-groups but less favorably than true in-groups

need for closure A stable individual trait based on the tendency toward urgency in finding an answer to any problem and the tendency toward the permanent adoption of that answer

normal retirement age The age at which people can claim full Social Security benefits

outcome expectations In social learning theory, the beliefs that a behavior leads to an outcome

out-group The group of which the individual does not consider him or herself a member

out-group hostility Unfriendliness or opposition to people in the out-group

parsimony A problem-solving approach that calls for choosing the simplest explanation that fits the evidence; sometimes called Occam's razor

partial youth culture Culture with a relatively young age demographic, but one that includes a substantial number of middle-aged and older adults

peripheral ageism A pattern of ageism in which the middle-aged are the advantaged group

persistent inequality hypothesis Hypothesis stating that inequality remains consistent as a person ages

political economy The study of the connections between politics, economics, and other systems of power

power distance The extent to which cultures expect and accept inequalities

preference reversals Change, in the opposite direction, of the relative frequency of preferences

primary frames More fundamental sets of rules and premises that serve as the basis for secondary frames

productive aging A term for engaging in socially productive activities such as volunteering, paid work, and caregiving in later life

proximal processes The interactions between the individual and those in their immediate environment

public pension programs Government programs that allot regular payments to the elderly

public pension systems Social Security and similar plans administered by the federal government

quality-adjusted life years (QALYs)   Measure that combines the years of life, adjusted for the quality of those years

reading history sideways   A logical fallacy in which we draw conclusions about the pre-literate societies of the distant past based on what we know about customs of present-day or recent cultures

reasonable factor other than age (RFOA)   Defense which, under the ADEA, allows employers to take age into account as long as they take into account other factors as well

redlining   (1) A practice of avoiding investment in neighborhoods with high proportions of racial minorities and (2) geographic discrimination, by which services are denied to residents based on the demographic composition of makeup of the area

relational demography   The study of the consequences of similarities and dissimilarities in demographic characteristics

replacement rate   The percentage of workers' income that their public pension benefits replace

reverse discrimination   Unfair or unequal treatment targeting younger people

secondary frames   Less fundamental sets of rules and premises built on top of primary frames

senior citizen discounts   A form of price discrimination in which businesses charge older adults less for goods and services, relative to younger adults

sex/gender system   In political economy, the ways in which gendered institutions, such as the state and families, transform biological sexuality into human activities

similarity-attraction hypothesis   A hypothesis stating that "birds of a feather flock together" or that similar individuals tend to view each other more positively

social identity theory   A theory of self-identity based on group membership

state   In political economy, the branches of government, the military, the criminal justice system, and public health, welfare, and educational institutions

stereotype buffering   Process by which one stereotype can buffer or protect a group from other stereotypes

stereotype content model   A theory that states that the content of stereotypes can be understood in terms of warmth (likeability, trustworthiness) and competence (intelligence, independence)

stereotype segmentation   The division of more general cultural stereotypes into a number of specific stereotype segments

stereotype threat   The threat of confirming or being judged according to a stereotype

subgrouping   The process through which people recognize that there are distinctions between subgroups within a larger group

substereotypes Stereotypes that apply to subgroups nested within a larger group

subtyping Process by which disconfirmers are clustered together mentally

succession ageism The set of cultural beliefs and assumptions about the proper age for older adults to make way for the younger generation

superordinate group Larger group within which subgroups are clustered

terror management theory A theory that argues that human culture functions to help us manage our fear of death

Title VII of the Civil Rights Act Federal law forbidding employment discrimination based on sex, race, color, national origin, and religion

unintentional Unfair or unequal treatment without conscious awareness

utilitarian ageism Ageism that arises due to the lower life expectancies of older people

value modernization framework A framework that links economic development and values, while recognizing enduring cultural and historical differences

well-being shift Shift from survival values to self-expression values, predicted by the value modernization framework

youth cultures The norms, activities, interests, and practices of youth

youth subcultures Cultural groupings within the larger youth culture

References

AARP. (2014). *Staying Ahead of the Curve 2013: Older Workers in an Uneasy Job Market*. Washington, DC: AARP Research. Retrieved from www.aarp.org/content/dam/aarp/research/surveys_statistics/general/2014/Staying-Ahead-of-the-Curve-2013-The-Work-and-Career-Study-AARP-res-gen.pdf

AARP. (2015). *A Business Case for Workers Age 50+: A Look at the Value of Experience*. Washington, DC: AARP Research. Retrieved from www.aarp.org/content/dam/aarp/research/surveys_statistics/general/2015/A-Business-Case-Report-for-Workers%20Age%2050Plus-res-gen.pdf

Abel, J. R., & Deitz, R. (2016). Underemployment in the Early Careers of College Graduates Following the Great Recession Federal Reserve Bank of New York Staff Report No. 749. Retrieved from www.newyorkfed.org/medialibrary/media/research/staff_reports/sr749.pdf?la=en

Abel, J. R., Deitz, R., & Su, Y. (2014). "Are recent college graduates finding good jobs?" *Current Issues in Economics and Finance*. Retrieved from www.newyorkfed.org/medialibrary/media/research/current_issues/ci20-1.pdf

Adler, G., & Rottunda, S. J. (2010). "Mandatory testing of drivers on the basis of age and degenerative diseases: Stakeholder opinions." *Journal of Aging and Social Policy*, 22: 304–319.

Adorno, T. W., Frenkel-Brunswik, E., Levinson, D. J., & Sanford, R. N. (1950). *The Authoritarian Personality*. New York: Harper and Row.

Age Discrimination in Employment Act. (1967). (Pub. L. 90–202), as amended, as it appears in volume 29 of the United States Code. Retrieved from www.eeoc.gov/laws/statutes/adea.cfm

Aggarwal, R., & Goodell, J. W. (2013). "Political-economy of pension plans: Impact of institutions, gender, and culture." *Journal of Banking and Finance*, 37: 1860–1879.

Allport, G. (1979). *The Nature of Prejudice*. New York: Perseus Books Publishing.

Arias, J. J. (2013). "A time to step in: Legal mechanisms for protecting those with declining capacity." *American Journal of Law and Medicine*, 39(2013): 134–159.

Ariew, R. (1976). *Ockham's Razor: A Historical and Philosophical Analysis of Ockham's Principle of Parsimony*. Champaign-Urbana, IL: University of Illinois.

Armstrong, B., Gallant, S. N., Li, L., Patel, K., & Wong, B. I. (2017). "Stereotype threat effects on older adults' episodic and working memory: A meta-analysis." *The Gerontologist*, 57(S2): S193–S205.

Arnett v. Aspin, 846 F. Supp. 1234 (E.D. Pa. 1994).

References

Arrow, K. J. (1973). "The theory of discrimination." In O. Ashenfelter & A. Rees (Eds), *Discrimination in Labor Markets*. Princeton, NJ: Princeton University Press.

Auerbach, A. J., Gokhale, J., & Kotlikoff, L. J. (1991). "Generational accounts: A meaningful alternative to deficit accounting." In D. F. Bradford (Ed.), *Tax Policy and the Economy*, Volume 5, pp. 55–110. Cambridge: MIT Press. Retrieved from www.nber.org/chapters/c11269

Autor, D. H., Katz, L. F., & Kearney, M. S. (2008). "Trends in U.S. wage inequality: Revising the revisionists." *Review of Economics and Statistics*, 90: 300–323.

Avey, J. B., West, B. J., & Crossley, C. D. (2008). "The association between ethnic congruence in the supervisor–subordinate dyad and subordinate organizational position and salary." *Journal of Occupational and Organizational Psychology*, 81: 551–566.

Baker, A. (1975). "Granny battering." *Modern Geriatric*, 8: 20–24.

Bandura, A. (1978). "Social learning theory of aggression." *Journal of Communication*, 28(3): 12–29.

Bandura, A., Ross, D., & Ross, S. A. (1961). "Transmission of aggression through imitation of aggressive models." *Journal of Abnormal and Social Psychology*, 63(3): 575–582.

Bandura, A., Ross, D., & Ross, S. A. (1963). "Imitation of film-mediated aggressive models." *Journal of Abnormal and Social Psychology*, 66(1): 3–11.

Barclay, L. (1982). "Social learning theory: A framework for discrimination research." *Academy of Management Review*, 7(4): 587–594.

Barrett, A. E., & Naiman-Sessions, M. (2016). "'It's our turn to play': Performance of girlhood as a collective response to gendered ageism." *Ageing and Society*, 36(4): 764–784.

Barry, L. C., Abou, J. J., Simen, A. A., & Gill, T. M. (2012). "Under-treatment of depression in older persons." *Journal of Affective Disorders*, 136(3): 780–796.

Baumle, A. K., & Fossett, M. (2005). "Statistical discrimination in employment: Its practice, conceptualization, and implications for public policy." *American Behavioral Scientist*, 48(9), 1250–1274.

Beal, F. M. (1969). *Double Jeopardy: To Be Black and Female*. New York: Third World Women's Alliance.

Beard, R. L., & Williamson, J. B. (2004). "Generational equity and generational interdependence: Framing of the debate over health and Social Security policy in the United States." *Indian Journal of Gerontology*, 18: 348–362.

Beard, R. L., & Williamson, J. B. (2016). "Frames matter: Aging policies and social disparities." *Public Policy and Aging Report*, 26(2): 48–52.

Beaudry, P., Green, D. A., & Sand, B. M.. (2014). "The declining fortunes of the young since 2000." *American Economic Review*, 104(5): 381–386.

Beaudry, P., Green, D. A., & Sand, B. M. (2016). "The great reversal in the demand for skill and cognitive tasks." *Journal of Labor Economics*, 34(S1–2): S199–S247.

Becker, E. (1973). *The Denial of Death*. New York: Free Press.

Becker, G. S. (1971 [1957]). *The Economics of Discrimination*. Chicago, IL: University of Chicago Press.

Bennett, A. (2006). "Punk's not dead: The continuing significance of punk rock for an older generation of fans." *Sociology*, 40(2): 219–235.

Bennett, A. (2018). "Popular music scenes and aging bodies." *Journal of Aging Studies*, 45: 49–53.

Benz, J., Sedensky, M., Thompson, T., & Agiesta, J. (2013). "Working longer: Older Americans' attitudes on work and retirement." *Associated Press* and *NORC*. Retrieved from www.apnorc.org/projects/Pages/working-longer-older-americans-attitudes-on-work-and-retirement.aspx

Berger, E. D. (2009). "Managing age discrimination: An examination of the techniques used when seeking employment." *The Gerontologist*, 49(3), 317–332. doi:10.1093/geront/gnp031

Bergman, Y. S., Bodner, E., & Cohen-Fridel, S. (2013). "Cross-cultural ageism: Ageism and attitudes toward aging among Jews and Arabs in Israel." *International Psychogeriatrics*, 25: 6–15.

Binney, E. A., Estes, C. L., & Ingman, S. R. (1990). "Medicalization, public policy and the elderly: Social services in jeopardy?" *Social Science and Medicine*, 30: 761–771.

Binstock, R. H. (1983). "The aged as scapegoat." *The Gerontologist*, 23: 136–143. doi:10.1093/geront/23.2.136

Binstock, R. H. (1999). "Scapegoating the old: Intergenerational equity and age-based health care rationing." In J. B. Williamson, E. R. Kingson, & D. M. Watts-Roy (Eds), *The Generational Equity Debate*, pp. 185–203. New York: Columbia University Press.

Binstock, R. H. (2010). "From compassionate ageism to intergenerational conflict?" *The Gerontologist*, 50(5): 574–585.

Blair-Loy, M. (2005). *Competing Devotions: Career and Family among Women Executives*. Cambridge, MA: Harvard University Press.

Blumberg, L. J., & Buettgens, M. (2013). "Why the ACA's limits on age-rating will not cause 'rate shock': Distributional implications of limited age bands in non-group heath insurance." Urban Institute Quick Strike Health Policy Analysis. Retrieved from www.rwjf.org/en/library/research/2013/03/why-the-aca-s-limits-on-age-rating-will-not-cause–rate-shock-.html

Boehm, S. A., & Swertmann, D. J. G. (2015). "Forging a single-edged sword: Facilitating positive age and disability diversity effects in the workplace through leadership, positive climates, and HR practices." *Work, Aging and Retirement*, 1(1): 41–63. doi:10.1093/workar/wau008

Bonnewyn, A., Katona, C., Bruffaerts, R., Haro, J. M., de Graaf, R., Alonso, J., & Demyttenaere, K. (2009). "Pain and depression in older people: Comorbidity and patterns of help seeking." *Journal of Affective Disorders*, 117: 193–196.

Botelho, L. A. (2004). *Old Age and the English Poor Law, 1500–1700*. Rochester, NY: Boydell Press.

Bowen, C. E., & Staudinger, U. M. (2013). "Relationship between age and promotion orientation depends on perceived older workers stereotypes." *Journals of Gerontology, Series B: Psychological Sciences and Social Sciences*, 68(1): 59–63. doi:10.1093/geronb/gbs060

Brewer, M. B., Dull, V., & Lui, L. (1981). "Perceptions of the elderly: Stereotypes as prototypes." *Journal of Personality and Social Psychology*, 41: 656–670.

Bronfenbrenner, U. (1977). "Toward an experimental ecology of human development." *American Psychologist*, 32: 515–531.

Bronfenbrenner, U. (1979). *The Ecology of Human Development: Experiments by Nature and Design*. Cambridge, MA: Harvard University Press.

Bronfenbrenner, U. (2000). "Ecological systems theory." In A. E. Kazdin (Ed.), *Encyclopedia of Psychology*, Vol. 3, pp. 129–133. Washington, DC: APA.

Bronfenbrenner, U. (1994). "Nature–nurture reconceptualized in developmental perspective: A bioecological model." *Psychological Review*, 101(4): 568–586.

Brown, T. H., O'Rand, A. M., & Adkins, D. E. (2012). "Race-ethnicity and health trajectories: Tests of three hypotheses across multiple groups and health outcomes." *Journal of Health and Social Behavior*, 53: 359–377. doi:10.1177/0022146512455333

Brownell, P. (2010). "Social issues and social policy response to abuse and neglect of older adults." In G. Gutman & C. Spencer (Eds), *Aging, Ageism, and Abuse: Moving from Awareness to Action*, pp. 1–15. London: Elsevier.

Brumberger, E., & Lauer, C. (2015). "The evolution of technical communication: An analysis of industry job postings." *Technical Communications*, 62(4): 224–243.

Brumley, K. M. (2014). "The gendered ideal worker narrative: Professional women's and men's work experiences in the new economy at a Mexican company." *Gender & Society*, 28(6): 799–823.

Burston, G. R. (1975). "Granny-battering." *British Medical Journal*, 3(5983): 592.

Byrne, D. E. (1971). *The Attraction Paradigm*. New York: Academic Press.

Cadinu, M., & Galdi, S. (2012). "Gender differences in implicit gender self-categorization lead to stronger gender self-stereotyping by women than by men." *European Journal of Social Psychology*, 42: 546–551.

Callahan, D. (1995). *Setting Limits: Medical Goals in an Aging Society*. Washington, DC: Georgetown University Press.

Cappelli, P. (2015). *Will College Pay Off? A Guide to the Most Important Financial Decision You'll Ever Make*. New York: Perseus Books Group.

Center on Aging & Work. (n.d.). "Innovative practices database." Retrieved from http://capricorn.bc.edu/agingandwork/database/search/case_study

Centers for Disease Control and Prevention. (2009). "Prevalence and most common causes of disability among adults: United States, 2005." *Morbidity and Mortality Weekly Report*, 58: 421–426. Washington, DC: Centers for Disease Control and Prevention.

Choi, J. N. (2006). "The role of derived rights for old-age income security of women." Social, Employment and Migration Working Papers No. 43.

Choi, J. N. (2007). "Group composition and employee creative behavior in a Korean electronics company: Distinct effects of relational demography and group diversity." *Journal of Occupational and Organizational Psychology*, 80: 213–234.

Civil Rights Act of 1964, Pub.L. 88–352, 78 Stat. 241(1964).

Clarke, L. H., Bennett, E. V., & Liu, C. (2014). "Aging and masculinity: Portrayals in men's magazines." *Journal of Aging Studies*, 31: 26–33.

Cohen-Cole, E. (2011). "Credit Card Redlining." *Review of Economics and Statistics*, 93: 700–713.

Collins, M. H., Hair, J. F., & Rocco, T. S. (2009). "The older-worker–younger-supervisor dyad: A test of the reverse Pygmalion effect." *Human Resource Development Quarterly*, 20: 21–41.

Connolly, M.-T. (2010). "Where elder abuse and the justice system collide: Police power, parens patriae, and 12 recommendations." *Journal of Elder Abuse and Neglect*, 22: 1–2, 37–93.

Conrad, P. (1992). "Medicalization and social control." *Annual Review of Sociology*, 18: 209–232.

Conrad, P. (2005). "The shifting engines of medicalization." *Journal of Health and Social Behavior*, 46(March): 3–14.

Cowgill, D. O. (1974). "Aging and modernization: A revision of the theory." In J. Gubrium (Ed.), *Late Life-Communities and Environmental Policy*, pp. 123–145. Springfield, IL: Charles C. Thomas.

Cowgill, D. O., & Holmes, L. D. (1972). *Aging and Modernization*. New York: Appleton-Century-Crofts.

Cuddy, A. J. C., & Fiske, S. T. (2002). "Doddering but dear: Process, content, and function in stereotyping of older persons." In T. D. Nelson (Ed.), *Ageism*, pp. 3–26. Cambridge, MA: MIT Press.

Cuddy, A. J. C., Norton, M. I., & Fiske, S. T. (2005). "This old stereotype: The stubbornness and pervasiveness of the elderly stereotype." *Journal of Social Issues*, 61: 265–283.

Daily Planet Staff. (2000). "Don't trust anyone over 30, unless it's Jack Weinberg." *Berkeley Daily Planet*. Retrieved from www.berkeleydailyplanet.com/issue/2000-04-06/article/759?headline=Don-t-trust-anyone-over-30-unless-it-s-Jack-Weinberg–Daily-Planet-Staff

Dannefer, D. (2003). "Cumulative advantage/disadvantage and the life course: Cross-fertilizing age and social science theory." *Journal of Gerontology: Social Sciences*, 58: S327–S337. doi:10.1093/geronb/58.6.S327

Davis, M. M.., Bond, L. A., Howard, A., & Sarkisian, C. A. "Primary care clinician expectations regarding Aging." *Gerontologist*, 51(5): 856–866.

Day, J. (2014). "Closing the loophole: Why intersectional claims are needed to address discrimination against older women." *Ohio State Law Journal*, 75(2): 447–476.

De Beauvoir, S. (1996 [1970]). *The Coming of Age*, trans. P. O'Brian. New York: W. W. Norton & Company.

De Pater, I. E., Judge, T. A., & Scott, B. A. (2014). "Age, gender, and compensation: A study of Hollywood movie stars." *Journal of Management Inquiry*, 23: 407–420. doi:10.1177/1056492613519861

Deal, J. J. (2006). *Retiring the Generation Gap: How Employees Young and Old Can Find Common Ground*. San Francisco, CA: John Wiley & Sons.

Diamond, J. (2012). *The World until Yesterday: What Can We Learn from Traditional Societies?* New York: Penguin.

Dobbin, F., Kalev, A., & Kelly, E. (2007). "Diversity management in corporate America." *Contexts*, 6(4): 21–27.

Dong, X., & Simon, M. A. (2011). "Enhancing national policy and programs to address elder abuse." *JAMA*, 305(23): 2460–2461.

Dordoni, P., & Argentero, P. (2015). "When age stereotypes are employment barriers: A conceptual analysis and a literature review on older workers stereotypes." *Ageing International*, 40: 393–412.

Drazen, A. (2000). *Political Economy in Macroeconomics*. Princeton, NJ: Princeton University Press.

Edsall, T. B. (2012). *The Age of Austerity: How Scarcity Will Remake American Politics*. New York: Doubleday.

Eisenstein, E. (1983). *The Printing Revolution in Early Modern Europe*. New York: Cambridge University Press.

Elder, G. H., Jr. (1994). "Time, human agency, and social change: Perspectives on the life course." *Social Psychology Quarterly*, 57: 4–15.

Esping-Andersen, G. (1999). *Social Foundations of Postindustrial Economics*. New York: Oxford University Press.

Estes, C. L. (1979). *The Aging Enterprise*. San Francisco, CA: Jossey-Bass.
Estes, C. L. (2001). "Political economy of aging: A theoretical framework." In *Social Policy and Aging: A Critical Perspective*, pp. 1–22. Thousand Oaks, CA: Sage.
Estes, C. L., Linkens, K. W., & Binney, E. A. (2001). "Critical perspectives on aging." In *Social Policy and Aging: A Critical Perspective*, pp. 23–44. Thousand Oaks, CA: Sage.
Fair Housing Act (42 U.S. Code § § 3601–3619 and 3631).
Fairlie, H. (1988). "Talkin' 'bout my generation." *New Republic*, March 28: 19–21.
Fang, H., & Moro, A. (2010). "Theories of statistical discrimination and affirmative action: A survey." NBER Working Paper 15860.
Farnum, K. S., & Wiener, R. L. (2016). "Stereotype content model, causal models, and allegations of age discrimination: Should the law change?" *Analysis of Social Issues and Public Policy*, 16(1): 100–124.
Ferraro, K. F., & Farmer, M. M. (1996). "Double jeopardy, aging as leveler, or persistent health inequality? A longitudinal analysis of white and black Americans." *Journal of Gerontology: Social Sciences*, 51B: S319–S328. doi:10.1093/geronb/51B.6.S319
Ferraro, K. F., & Shippee, T. P. (2009). "Aging and cumulative inequality: How does inequality get under the skin?" *The Gerontologist*, 49, 334. doi:10.1093/geront/gnp034
Fiske, S. T., Xu, J., Cuddy, A. C., & Glick, P. (1999). "(Dis)respecting versus (dis)liking: Status and interdependence predict ambivalent stereotypes of competence and warmth." *Journal of Social Issues*, 55: 472–489.
Friedberg, L. (2000). "The labor supply effects of the social security earnings test." *Review of Economics and Statistics*, 82: 48–63.
Gage, F. D. (1881). "Reminiscences by Frances D. Gage: Sojourner truth." In E. C. Stanton, S. B. Anthony, & M. J. Gage (Eds), *History of Woman Suffrage*, Vol. 1. Rochester, NY: Susan B. Anthony, Charles Mann.
Galston, W. A. (2014). "Welcome to the well-educated-barista economy." *Wall Street Journal*, April 29.
Gamson, W. A., & Modigliani, A. (1987). "The changing culture of affirmative action." In R. G. Braungart & M. M. Braungart (Eds), *Research in Political Sociology*, Vol. 3, pp. 137–177. Greenwich, CT: JAI Press.
Gamson, W. A., & Modigliani, A. (1989). "Media discourse and public opinion on nuclear power: A constructionist approach." *American Journal of Sociology*, 95(1): 1–37.
General Dynamics Land Systems, Inc. v. Cline, 540 U.S. 581 (2004).
Gerbner, G. (2000). "Cultivation analysis: An overview." *Communicator*, October–December: 3–12.
Gerbner, G., Gross, L., Signorielli, N., & Morgan, M. (1980). "Television violence, victimization, and power." *American Behavioral Scientist*, 23(5): 705–716.
Ghent, A. C. (2010). "Residential mortgage renegotiation during the Great Depression." Retrieved from www.fdic.gov/bank/analytical/cfr/mortgage_future_house_finance/papers/ghent.pdf
Giles, H., & Ogay, T. (2006). "Communication accommodation theory." In B. B. Whaley & W. Samter (Eds), *Explaining Communication: Contemporary Theories and Exemplars*, pp. 325–344. New York: Routledge.
Givskov, C., & Petersen, L. N. (2018). "Media and the ageing body: Introduction to the special issue." *European Journal of Cultural Studies*, 21(3): 281–289.

Glater, J. D. (2015). "Student debt and higher education risk." *California Law Review*, 103(6): 1561–1714.

Glick, P., & Fiske, S. T. (1996). "The ambivalent sexism inventory: Differentiating hostile and benevolent sexism." *Journal of Personality and Social Psychology*, 70: 491–512.

Goffman, E. (1963). *Stigma: Notes on the Management of Spoiled Identity*. Englewood Cliffs, NJ: Prentice-Hall.

Goffman, E. (1974). *Frame Analysis: An Essay on the Organization of Experience*. Boston, MA: Northeastern University Press.

Goh, J. X., & Hall, J. A. (2015). "Nonverbal and verbal expressions of men's sexism in mixed-gender interactions." *Sex Roles*, 72: 252–261.

Gokhale, J. (2012). "Fiscal and generational imbalances and generational accounts: A 2012 update." Cato Institute Working Paper, November. Retrieved from www.cato.org/publications/working-paper/fiscal-generational-imbalances-generational-accounts-2012-update

Goldberg, C. B., Riordan, C., & Schaffer, B. S. (2010). "Does social identity theory underlie relational demography? A test of the moderating effects of uncertainty reduction and status enhancement on similarity effects." *Human Relations*, 63: 903–926.

Grabowski, D. C., Campbell, C. M., & Morrisey, M. A. (2004). "Elderly Licensure Laws and Motor Vehicle Fatalities." *Journal of the American Medical Association*, 291: 2840–2846.

Graetz, I., Kaplan, C. M., Kaplan, E. K., Bailey, J. E., & Waters, T. M. (2014). "The U.S. health insurance marketplace: Are premiums truly affordable?" *Annals of Internal Medicine*, 161: 599–604.

Green, K. K. (2004). "A reason to discriminate: Curtailing the use of Title VII analysis in claims arising under the ADEA." *Louisiana Law Review*, 65(1): 411–442.

Greenwald, A. G., McGhee, D. E., & Schwartz, J. K. L. (1998). "Measuring individual differences in implicit cognition: The Implicit Association Test." *Journal of Personality and Social Psychology*, 74: 1464–1480.

Gross v. FBL Financial Services Inc., 557 U.S. 167 (2009).

Haas, S., & Rohlfsen, L. (2010). "Life course determinants of racial and ethnic disparities in functional health trajectories." *Social Science and Medicine*, 70: 240–250. doi:10.1016/j.socscimed.2009.10.003

Hacker, J. S. (2006). *The Great Risk Shift: The New Economic Insecurity and the Decline of the American Dream*. New York: Oxford University Press.

Hacker, J. S. (2011). "Restoring retirement security: The market crisis, the 'great risk shift,' and the challenge for our nation." *Elder Law Journal*, 19(1): 1–48.

Hall, D. T. (2002). *Careers in and out of Organizations*. Thousand Oaks, CA: Sage.

Harper, M. C. (2012). "Reforming the Age Discrimination in Employment Act: Proposals and prospects." *Employee Rights and Employment Policy Journal*, 16(1): 13–49.

Harris, J. (1985). *The Value of Life*. London: Routledge.

Harwell, D. (2012). "8-year old can stay in grandparents' age-restricted neighborhood, judge rules." *Tampa Bay Times*, May 15. Retrieved from www.tampabay.com/news/humaninterest/judge-ends-long-legal-battle-8-year-old-can-stay-in-clearwater-adults-only/1230107

Hehman, J. A., & Bugental, D. B. (2015). "Responses to patronizing communication and factors that attenuate those responses." *Psychology and Aging*, 30(3): 552–560.

Held, D. (1980). *Introduction to Critical Theory: Horkheimer to Habermas*. Berkeley, CA: University of California Press.

Henneberg, S. (2010). "Moms do badly, but grandmas do worse: The nexus of sexism and ageism in children's classics." *Journal of Aging Studies*, 24: 125–134.

Hetsroni, A. (2012). "Associations between television viewing and love styles: An interpretation using cultivation theory." *Psychological Reports*, 110(1): 35–50.

Hightower, J. (2010). "Abuse in later life: When and how does gender matter?" In G. Gutman & C. Spencer (Eds), *Aging, Ageism, and Abuse: Moving from Awareness to Action*, pp. 17–29. New York: Elsevier.

Hodkinson, P. (2012). "Family and parenthood in an ageing 'youth' culture: A collective embrace of dominant adulthood." *Sociology*, 47(6): 1072–1087.

Hofstede, G., Hofstede, G. J., & Minkov, M. (1993). *Cultures and Organizations: Software of the Mind*, 3rd edn. New York: McGraw Hill.

Horton, S., Baker, J., Pearce, W., & Deakin, J. M. (2010). "Immunity to popular stereotypes of aging? Seniors and stereotype threat." *Educational Gerontology*, 36(5): 353–371.

Housing for Older Persons Act (Pub.L. 104–176, 109 Stat. 787).

Hudson, R. B. (1978). "The 'graying' of the federal budget and its consequences for old age policy." *The Gerontologist*, 18: 428–440.

Hugenberg, K., & Bodenhausen, G. V. (2003). "Facing prejudice: Implicit prejudice and the perception of facial threat." *Psychological Science*, 14: 640–643.

Hughes, J. (2005). "Palliative care and the QALY problem." *Health Care Analysis*, 13(4): 289–301.

Inglehart, R., & Baker, W. E. (2000). "Modernization, cultural chance and the persistence of traditional values." *American Sociological Review*, 64(1): 19–51.

Inglehart, R., & Welzel, C. (2005). *Modernization, Cultural Change, and Democracy: The Human Development Sequence*. New York: Cambridge University Press.

Insurance Institute for Highway Safety. (2015). "Older drivers." Retrieved from www.iihs.org/iihs/topics/laws/olderdrivers

Jamieson, P. E., & Romer, D. (2014). "Violence in popular U.S. prime time TV dramas and the cultivation of fear: A time series analysis." *Media and Communication*, 2(2): 31–41.

Janssen, J., Deschesne, M., & Van Knippenberg, A. (1999). "The psychological importance of youth culture: A terror management approach." *Youth and Society*, 31(2): 152–167.

Jeffries v. HarrisCounty Community Action Association, 425 F. Supp. 1208 (S.D. Tex. 1977).

Johnson, K. J., & Mutchler, J. E. (2013). "The emergence of a positive gerontology: From disengagement to social involvement." *The Gerontologist*, 54(1): 93–100.

Johnson, L. B. (1967). "Public papers of the presidents of the United States: Lyndon B. Johnson 1967, January 1 to June 30, 1967." Washington, DC: U.S. Government Printing Office.

Jonas, E., & Fischer, P. (2006). "Terror management and religion: Evidence that intrinsic religiousness mitigates worldview defense following mortality salience." *Journal of Personality and Social Psychology*, 91: 553–567.

Joseph, J. (2001 [1962]). *Warning: When I Am an Old Woman I Shall Wear Purple*. London: Souvenir Press.

Kaelber, W. O. (2004). "Āśrama." In S. Mittal & G. Thursby (Eds), *The Hindu World*, pp. 383–406. New York: Routledge.

Kang, S. K., & Chasteen, A. L. (2009). "Beyond the double-jeopardy hypothesis: The faces of multiply-categorizable targets of prejudice." *Journal of Experimental Social Psychology*, 45: 1281–1285.

Karnieli-Miller, O., Werner, P., Neufeld-Kroszynski, G., & Eidelman, S. (2012). "Are you talking to me?! An exploration of the triadic physician-patient-companion communication within memory clinic encounters." *Patient Education and Counseling*, 88: 381–390.

Kaufmann, M. C., Krings, F., & Sczesny, S. (2016). "Looking too old? How an older age appearance reduces chances of being hired." *British Journal of Management*, 27(4): 727–739.

Kearney, E., & Gebert, D. (2009). "Managing diversity and enhancing team outcomes: The promise of transformational leadership." *Journal of Applied Psychology*, 94(1): 77–89.

Kemper, S., & Harden, T. (1999). "Experimentally disentangling what's beneficial about elderspeak from what's not." *Psychology and Aging*, 14: 656–670.

Kerr, C., Dunlop, J., Harbison, F., & Myers, C. (1960). *Industrialism and Industrial Man*. Cambridge, MA: Harvard University Press.

Khan, R. J., & Jain, D. C. (2005). "An empirical analysis of price discrimination mechanisms and retailer profitability." *Journal of Marketing Research*, 42: 516–524.

King, D. K. (1988). "Multiple jeopardy, multiple consciousness: The context of a black feminist ideology." *Signs*, 14: 42–72.

Kingson, E. R., Hirshorn, B. A., & Cornman, J. M. (1986). *Ties that Bind: The Interdependence of Generations*. Seven Locks Press.

Kosberg, J. I. (2010). "The invisible problem of abused older men." In G. Gutman & C. Spencer (Eds), *Aging, Ageism, and Abuse: Moving from Awareness to Action*, pp. 31–43. New York: Elsevier.

Krieger, T., & Traub, S. (2013). "The Bismarckian factor: A measure of intragenerational redistribution in international pension systems." *CESifo DICE Rep*, 11(1): 64–66.

Kruglanski, A. W. (1989). *Lay Epistemics and Human Knowledge: Cognitive and Motivational Bases*. New York: Springer.

Lachs, M. S., & Pillemer, K. (2004). "Elder abuse." *Lancet*, 364: 1263–1272.

Lahey, J. N. (2008). "Age, women, and hiring: An experimental study." *Journal of Human Resources*, 153: 30–56.

Laidsaar-Powell, R. C., Butow, P. N., Bu, S., Charles, C., Gafni, A., Lam, W. W. T., Jansen, J., McCaffery, K. J., Shepherd, H. L., Tattersall, M. H. N., & Juraskova, I. (2013). "Physician-patient-companion communication and decision-making: A systematic review of triadic medical consultations." *Patient Education and Counseling*, 91: 3–13.

Lamb, S. (2000). *White Saris and Sweet Mangos: Aging, Gender, and Body in North India*. Berkeley, CA: University of CA Press.

Lamb, S. (2009). *Aging and the Indian Diaspora: Cosmopolitan Families in India and Abroad*. Bloomington, IN: Indiana University Press.

Lashbrook, J. (1996). "Promotional timetables: An exploratory investigation of age norms for promotional expectations and their association with job well-being." *The Gerontologist*, 36: 189–198. doi:10.1093/geront/36.2.189

Latrofa, M., Vaes, J., & Cadinu, M. (2012). "Self-stereotyping: The central role of an ingroup threatening identity." *Journal of Social Psychology*, 152(1): 92–111.

Laughey, D. (2006). *Music and Youth Culture*. Edinburgh: Edinburgh University Press.

Lazear, E. P. (1979). "Why is there mandatory retirement?" *Journal of Political Economy*, 87: 1261–1284.

Lee, C.-J., & Niederdeppe, J. (2011). "Genre-specific cultivation effects: Lagged associations between overall TV viewing, local TV news viewing, and fatalistic beliefs about cancer prevention." *Communication Research*, 38(6): 731–753.

Leroux, M.-L., & Pestieau, P. (2011). "The political economy of derived pension rights." *International Tax and Publix Finance*, 19(5): 753–776.

Levy, B. R., Chung, P. H., Bedford, T., & Navrazhina, K. (2013). "Facebook as a site for negative age stereotypes." *The Gerontologist*, 54(2): 172–176.

Levy, R., & Banaji, M. R. (2002). "Implicit ageism." In T. D. Nelson (Ed.), *Ageism: Stereotyping and Prejudice against Older Persons*. Cambridge, MA: MIT Press.

Lincoln, A. E., & Allen, M. P. (2004). "Double jeopardy in Hollywood: Age and gender in the careers of film actors, 1926–1999." *Sociological Forum*, 19: 611–631.

Lombardi, N. J., Buchanan, J. A., Afflerbach, S., Campana, K., Sattler, A., & Lai, D. (2014). "Is elderspeak appropriate? A survey of certified nursing assistants." *Journal of Gerontological Nursing*, 11: 44–52.

Luo, Y., Xu, J., Granberg, E., & Wentworth, W. M. (2012). "A longitudinal study of social status, perceived discrimination, and physical and emotional health among older adults." *Research on Aging*, 34: 275–301.

MacDorman, M. F., Matthews, T. J., & Declercq, E. (2014). "Trends in out-of-hospital births in the United States, 1990–2012." *NCHS Data Brief*, 144.

Macnicol, J. (2006). *Age Discrimination: A Historical and Contemporary Analysis*. New York: Cambridge University Press.

Marks v. LoralCorporation. California Court of Appeal, Fourth District, Division 3. (1997). Retrieved from https://caselaw.findlaw.com/ca-court-of-appeal/1122261.html

Marshall, B. (2015). "Anti-ageing and identity." In K. Twigg & W. Martin (Eds), *Routledge Handbook of Cultural Gerontology*, pp. 210–17. New York: Routledge.

Marshall, B. L., & Rahman, M. (2014). "Celebrity, ageing, and the construction of 'third age' identities." *International Journal of Cultural Studies*, 18(6): 577–593.

Martens, A., Greenberg, J., Schimel, J., & Landau, M. J. (2004). "Ageism and death: Effects of mortality salience and similarity to elders on distancing from and derogation of elderly people." *Personality and Social Psychology Bulletin*, 30: 1524–1536.

Martens, A., Goldenberg, J. L., & Greenberg, J. (2005). "A terror management perspective on ageism." *Journal of Social Issues*, 61(2): 223–239.

Matz-Costa, T. (2012). "The ideal worker vs. the older worker." Retrieved from http://agingandwork.bc.edu/blog/the-ideal-worker-vs-the-older-worker/

Maurer, K. L., Park, B., & Rothbart, M. (1995). "Subtyping versus subgrouping processes in stereotype representation." *Journal of Personality and Social Psychology*, 69: 812–824.

McConatha, J. T., Schnell, F., Volkwein, K., Riley, L., & Leach, E. (2003). "Attitudes toward aging: A comparative analysis of young adults from the United States and Germany." *International Journal of Aging and Human Development*, 57: 203–215.

McNally, M. D. (2009). *Honoring Elders: Aging, Authority, and Ojibwe Religion*. New York: Columbia University Press.

McNamara, T. K., Sano, J., & Williamson, J. B. (2012). "The pros and cons of pro-work policies and programs for older workers." In J. W. Hedge & W. C. Borman (Eds), *Oxford Handbook of Work and Aging*, pp. 663–686. New York: Oxford University Press.

Menger, K. (1979). *Selected Papers in Logic and Foundations, Didactics, Economics*. Boston, MA: D. Reidel Publishing Company.

Merton, R. K. (1968). "The Matthew effect in science: The reward and communication systems of science are considered." *Science*, 159(3810): 56–63.

Metlife Mature Market Institute & National Association of Home Builders. (2011). *Housing Trends Update for the 55+ Market: New Insights from the American Housing Survey*.

Mill, J. S. (1848). *Principles of Political Economy*. New York: D. Appleton & Company.

Milliken, F. J., & Martins, L. L. (1996). "Searching for common threads: Understanding the multiple effects of diversity in organizational groups." *Academy of Management Review*, 21: 402–433.

Monge-Naranjo, A., & Sohail, F. (2015). "The composition of long-term unemployment is changing toward older workers." *Regional Economist*. Retrieved from www.stlouisfed.org/~/media/Publications/Regional-Economist/2015/October/unemployment.pdf

Morganroth Gullette, M. (2010). *Agewise*. Chicago, IL: University of Chicago Press.

Morrow-Howell, N., Gonzales, E., Matz-Costa, C., & Greenfield, E. A. (2015). *Increasing Productive Engagement in Later Life*. Grand Challenges for Social Work Initiative Working Paper No. 8. Cleveland, OH: American Academy of Social Work and Social Welfare. Retrieved from http://aaswsw.org/wp-content/uploads/2015/03/Productive-Engagement-3.24.151.pdf

Morrow-Howell, N., Gonzales, E. G., Harootyan, R. A., Lee, Y., & Lindberg, B. W. (2017). "Approaches, Policies, and Practices to Support the Productive Engagement of Older Adults." *Journal of Gerontological Social Work*, 60(3): 193–200.

Munnell, A. H., & Wu, A. Y. (2013). "SIEPR Discussion Paper No. 13–011." Stanford, CA: Stanford Institute for Economic Policy Research. Retrieved from http://siepr.stanford.edu/sites/default/files/publications/Do.older_.workers.squeeze.out_.younger.workers_2.pdf

Munnell, A. H., Hou, W., & Webb, A. (2014). "NRRI update shows half still falling short." Report No. 14–20. Chestnut Hill, MA: Center for Retirement Research at Boston College. Retrieved from http://crr.bc.edu/wp-content/uploads/2014/12/IB_14-20-508.pdf

Myles, J., & Quadagno, J. (2002). "Political theories of the welfare state." *Social Service Review*, 76(1): 34–57.

Nelson, T. D. (2011). "Ageism: The strange case of prejudice against the older you." In R. L. Wiener & S. L. Willborn (Eds), *Disability and Aging Discrimination*, pp. 37–47. New York: Springer.

Neumark, D. (2003). "Age discrimination legislation in the United States." *Contemporary Economic Policy*, 21(3): 297–317.

Neumark, D. (2010). "Detecting discrimination in audit and correspondence studies." NBER Working Paper 16447.

Neumark, D., Burn, I., & Button, P. (2016). "Is it harder for older workers to find jobs? New and improved evidence from a field experiment." NBER Working Paper 21669.

Normand, C. (2009). "Measuring outcomes in palliative care: Limitations of WALYs and the road to PalYs." *Journal of Pain and Symptom Management*, 38: 27–31.

North, M. S., & Fiske, S. T. (2013). "Subtyping ageism: Policy issues in succession and consumption." *Social Issues and Policy Review*, 7(1): 36–57.

O'Berg, C. (2003). "The impact of childhood poverty on health and development." *Healthy Generations*, 4: 1–3.

O'Brien, L. T., & Hummert, M. L. (2006). "Memory performance of late middle-aged adults: Contrasting self-stereotyping and stereotype threat accounts of assimilation to age stereotypes." *Social Cognition*, 24(3): 338–358.

O'Connor, M. L., & McFadden, S. H. (2012). "A terror management perspective on young adults' ageism and attitudes toward dementia." *Educational Gerontology*, 38: 627–643.

O'Rand, A. M. (1996). "The precious and the precocious: Understanding cumulative disadvantage and cumulative advantage over the life course." *The Gerontologist*, 36: 230–238.

Ouchida, K. M., & Lachs, M. S. (2015). "Not for doctors only: Ageism in healthcare. Generations." Retrieved from asaging.org/blog/not-doctors-only-ageism-healthcare

Painter, N. I. (1996). *Sojourner Truth: A Life, a Symbol*. New York: W. W. Norton & Company.

Palmore, E. (1999). *Ageism: Negative and Positive*, 2nd edn. New York: Springer.

Parsons, T. (1960). *Structure and Process in Modern Societies*. New York: Free Press.

Parsons, T. (1972). "Age and sex in the social structure of the United States." *American Sociological Review*, 7: 604–616.

Phelps, E. S. (1972). "The statistical theory of racism and sexism." *American Economic Review*, 62: 659–661.

Phillips v. MartinMarietta Corp., 400 U.S. 542 (1971).

Polygraph. (2016). "Filmplay dialogue from 2,000 screenplays, broken down by gender and age." Retrieved from http://polygraph.cool/films/

Porter, N. B. (2003). "Sex plus age discrimination: Protecting older women." *Denver University Law Review*, 81(1): 79–111.

Posthuma, R. A., & Campion, M. A. (2009). "Age stereotypes in the workplace: Common stereotypes, moderators, and future research directions." *Journal of Management*, 23(1), 158–188. doi:10.1177/0149206308318617

Potter, W. J. (2014). "A critical analysis of cultivation theory." *Journal of Communication*, 64: 1015–1036.

Preston, S. H. (1984). "Children and the elderly: Divergent paths for America's dependents." *Demography*, 21(4): 435–457.

Project Implicit. (2011). Retrieved from www.projectimplicit.net/index.html

Quadagno, J. B. (1989). "Generational equity and the politics of the welfare state." *Politics and Society*, 17(3): 353–376.

Rafalow, M. H. (2018). "Disciplining play: Digital youth culture as capital at school." *American Journal of Sociology*, 123(5): 1416–1452.

Ratcliffe, C., & McKernan, S. (2010). "Childhood poverty persistence: Facts and consequences (Brief No. 14)." Washington, DC: Urban Institute. Retrieved from www.urban.org/UploadedPDF/412126-child-poverty-persistence.pdf

Reid, E. (2015). "Embracing, passing, revealing, and the ideal worker image: How people navigate expected and experienced professional identities." *Organization Science*, 26(4): 997–1017.

Renvoize, J. (1976). "Granny bashing." *Guardian*, February 5: 9.

Ricci et al. v. Destedano et al. (2009). Retrieved from www.supremecourt.gov/opinions/08pdf/07-1428.pdf

Richards, Z., & Hewstone, M. (2001). "Subtyping and subgrouping: Processes for the prevention and promotion of stereotype change." *Personality and Social Psychology Review*, 5: 52–73.

Rittel, H. W. J., & Webber, M. M. (1973). "Dilemmas in a General Theory of Planning." *Policy Sciences*, 4(2): 155–169.

Rivera-Roso, J. A., García-Huitrón, M. E., Steenbeek, O. W., & van der Lecq, S. G. (2018). "National culture and the configuration of public pensions." *Journal of Comparative Economics*, 46: 457–479.

Roberto, K. A. (2016). "The complexities of elder abuse." *American Psychologist*, 71(4): 302–311.

Robinson, T., & Anderson, C. (2006). "Older characters in children's animated television programs: A content analysis of their portrayal." *Journal of Broadcasting and Electronic Media*, 50(2): 287–304.

Roets, A., & Van Hiel, A. (2011). "Allport's prejudiced personality today: Need for closure as the motivated cognitive basis of prejudice." *Current Directions in Psychological Science*, 20: 349–354.

Rosenblatt, A., Greenberg, J., Solomon, S.Pyszczynski, T., & Lyon, D. (1989). "Evidence for terror management theory: The effects of mortality salience on reactions to those who violate or uphold cultural values." *Journal of Personality and Social Psychology*, 57: 681–690.

Roth, E. G., Keimig, L., Rubinstein, R. L., Morgan, L., Ekert, J. K., Goldman, S., & Peeples, A. D. (2012). "Baby Boomers in an active adult retirement community: Comity interrupted." *The Gerontologist*, 52: 189–198.

Rothenberg, J. Z., & Gardner, D. A. (2011). "Protecting older workers: The failure of the age discrimination in employment act of 1967." *Journal of Sociology and Social Welfare*, 38(1): 9–30.

Rutledge, M. S., Gillis, C. M., & Webb, A. (2015). "Will the average retirement age continue to increase?" Center for Retirement Research WP 2015–2016. Retrieved from http://crr.bc.edu/wp-content/uploads/2015/07/wp_2015-16.pdf

Ryan, E. B., Kennaly, D. E., Pratt, M. W., & Shumovich, M. A. (2000). "Evaluations by staff, residents, and community seniors of patronizing speech in the nursing home: Impact of passive, assertive, or humorous responses." *Psychology and Aging*, 15: 272–285.

Saad-Lessler, J., Ghilarducci, T., & Bahn, K. (2015). "Are U.S. workers ready for retirement? Trends in plan sponsorship, participation, and preparedness." New York: Schwartz Center for Economic Policy Analysis, New School. Retrieved from www.economicpolicyresearch.org/images/docs/research/retirement_security/Are_US_Workers_Ready_for_Retirement.pdf

Sagawa, S., & Segal, E. (2000). *Common Interest, Common Good: Creating Value through Business and Social Sector Partnerships*. Boston, MA: Harvard Business School University Press.

Salomon, K., Burgess, K. D., & Bosson, J. K. (2015). "Flash fire and slow burn: Women's cardiovascular reactivity and recovery following hostile and benevolent sexism." *Journal of Experimental Psychology: General*, 144: 469–479.

Savishinsky, J. S. (2000). *Breaking the Watch: The Meanings of Retirement in America*. Ithaca, NY: Cornell University.

Scharrer, E., & Blackburn, G. (2018). "Is reality TV a bad girls club? Television use, docusoap reality television viewing, and the cultivation of approval of aggression." *Journalism and Mass Communication Quarterly*, 95(1): 235–257.

Schermuly, C., Deller, J., & Busch, V. (2014). "A research note on age discrimination and the desire to retire: The Mediating effect of psychological empowerment." *Research on Aging* 36(3): 382–393.

Scheufele, D. A., & Tewksbury, D. (2007). "Framing, agenda setting, and priming: The evolution of three media effects models." *Journal of Communication*, 57(1): 9–20.

Scholes, V. (2014). "You are not worth the risk: Lawful discrimination in hiring." *Rationality, Markets and Morals*, 5: 13–29.

Seavoy, R. (2006). *An Economic History of the United Sates from 1607 to the Present*. New York: Routledge.

Sherif, M. (1958). "Superordinate goals in the reduction of intergroup conflict." *American Journal of Sociology*, 63: 349–356.

SHRM. (2015). *The Aging Workforce-Basic and Applied Skills*. Washington, DC: Society for Human Resource Management. Retrieved from www.shrm.org/research/surveyfindings/articles/pages/shrm-older-workers-basic-and-applied-skills.aspx

SHRM. (2016). *The New Talent Landscape: Recruiting Difficulty and Skills Shortages*. Retrieved from www.shrm.org/hr-today/trends-and-forecasting/research-and-surveys/Documents/SHRM%20New%20Talent%20Landscape%20Recruiting%20Difficulty%20Skills.pdf

Shroyen, S., Adam, S., Marquet, M., Jersulem, G., Thiel, S., Giraudet, A. L., & Missotten, P. (2017). "Communication of healthcare professionals: Is there ageism?" *European Journal of Cancer Care*, 27: e12780.

Shrum, L. J., Lee, J., Burroughs, J. E., & Rindfleisch, A. (2011). "An online process model of second-order cultivation effects: How television cultivates materialism and its consequences for life satisfaction." *Human Communications Research*, 37: 34–57.

Smith, A. (1776). *An Inquiry into the Nature and Causes of the Wealth of Nations*. Retrieved from www.econlib.org/library/Smith/smWN.html?chapter_num=1#book-reader

Smith, A., & Anderson, M. (2018). "Social media use in 2018." Pew Research Center Report. Retrieved from www.pewinternet.org/2018/03/01/social-media-use-in-2018/

Smith, W. (1956). "Product differentiation and market segmentation as alternative marketing strategies." *Journal of Marketing*, 21(1): 3–8.

Snape, E., & Redman, T. (2003). "Too old or too young? The impact of perceived age discrimination." *Human Resource Management Journal*, 13(1): 78–89. doi:10.1111/j.1748–8583.2003.tb00085.x

Snethen, G., & Van Puymbroeck, M. (2008). "Girls and physical aggression: Causes, trends, and intervention guided by social learning theory." *Aggression and Violent Behavior*, 13: 346–354.

Social Security Administration. (n.d.). "Exempt amounts under the earnings test." Retrieved from www.ssa.gov/oact/cola/rtea.html

Solomon, S., Greenberg, J., & Pyszczynski, T. (2015). *The Worm at the Core: On the Role of Death in Life*. New York: Random House.

Song, J. (2013). "Falling between the cracks: Discrimination laws and older women." Unpublished paper. Irvine, CA: University of California.

Song, J., & Manchester, J. (2007). "New evidence on earnings and benefit claims following changes in the retirement earnings test in 2000." *Journal of Public Economics*, 91(3–4): 669–700.

Sprogis v. *UnitedAir Lines*, 444 F.2d 1194 (7th Cir. 1971).

Steele, C. M., & Aronson, J. (1995). "Stereotype threat and the intellectual test performance of African Americans." *Journal of Personality and Social Psychology*, 69(5): 797–811.

Super, D. E. (1990). "A life-span, life-space approach to career development." In D. Brown & L. Brook (Eds), *Career Choice and Development*, 2nd edn, pp. 197–261. San Francisco, CA: Jossey Bass.

Superior Court of Pennsylvania. (2012). "Health Care and Retirement Corporation of America, d/b/a/ Liberty Nursing and Rehabilitation Center, Appellee v. John PITTAS, Incorrectly Identified as John Pettas, Appellant." Retrieved from http://caselaw.findlaw.com/pa-superior-court/1607095.html

Swetz, F. J. (1987). *Capitalism and Arithmetic: The New Math of the 15th Century—Including the Full Text of the Treviso Arithmetic of 1478*. La Salle, IL: Open Court.

Tajfel, H., & Turner, J. C. (1979). "An integrative theory of intergroup conflict." In W. G. Austin & S. Worchel (Eds), *The Social Psychology of Intergroup Relations*. Monterey, CA: Brooks-Cole.

Tajfel, H., Billig, M. G., Bundy, R. P., & Flament, C. (1971). "Social categorization and intergroup behaviour." *European Journal of Social Psychology*, 1: 149–178.

Thornton, A. (2005). *Reading History Sideways: The Fallacy and Enduring Impact of the Developmental Paradigm on Family Life*. Chicago, IL: University of Chicago Press.

Title VII of the Civil Rights Act of 1964 (Pub. L. 88–352).

Townsend, P. (1981). "The structured dependency of the elderly: A creation of social policy in the twentieth century." *Ageing and Society*, 1(1): 5–28.

Treuer, A. (2010). *Ojibwe in Minnesota*. Ann Arbor, MI: Sheridan Books.

Trolander, J. A. (2011). "Age 55 or better: Active adult communities and city planning." *Journal of Urban History*, 37: 952–974.

Truxillo, D. M., McCune, E. A., Bertolino, M., & Fraccaroli, F. (2012). "Perceptions of older versus younger workers in terms of big five facets, proactive personality, cognitive ability, and job performance." *Journal of Applied Psychology*, 42(11): 2607–2639.

Tsuchiya, A. (2000). "QALYs and ageism: Philosophical theories and age weighting." *Health Economics*, 9: 57–68.

Tsuchiya, A., Dolan, P., & Shaw, R. (2003). "Measuring people's preference regarding ageism in health: Some methodological issues and some fresh evidence." *Social Science and Medicine*, 57: 687–696.

Tsui, A. S., & O'Reilly, C. A. (1989). "Beyond simple demographic effects: The importance of relational demography in superior-subordinate dyads." *Academy of Management Journal*, 32: 402–423.

Tsui, A. S., Egan, T. D., & O'Reilly, C. A. (1992). "Being different: Relational demography and organizational attachment." *Administrative Science Quarterly*, 37: 549–579.

Tversky, A., & Kahneman, D. (1981). "The framing of decisions and the psychology of choice." *Science*, 211(4481): 453–458.

Twigg, J. (2018). "Fashion, the media and age: How women's magazines use fashion to negotiate age identities." *European Journal of Cultural Studies*, 21(3): 334–348.

United States Government Accountability Office. (2015). "Retirement security: Most households approaching retirement have low savings." Retrieved from www.gao.gov/assets/680/670153.pdf

U.S. Census Bureau, Statistical Abstract of the United States. (2012). 131st edn. Washington, DC. Retrieved from www.census.gov/compendia/statab/

U.S. Department of Health and Human Services. (2017). "Health, United States, 2016." Washington, DC: U.S. Government Printing Office.

Van der Heijden, B. I. J. M., Scholarios, D., Jedrzejowicz, P., Bozionelos, N., Epitropaki, O., Knauth, P., & Van Der Heijde, C. (2010). "Supervisor-subordinate age dissimilarity and performance ratings: The buffering effects of supervisory relationships and practice." *International Journal of Aging and Human Development*, 71: 231–258.

Vanden Abeele, M. M. P. (2016). "Mobile lifestyles: Conceptualizing heterogeneity in mobile youth culture." *New Media and Society*, 18(6): 908–926.

Webster, D. M., & Kruglanski, A. W. (1994). "Individual differences in need for cognitive closure." *Journal of Personality and Social Psychology*, 67(6): 1049–1062.

Willerslev, R. (2009). "The optimal sacrifice: A study of voluntary death among the Siberian Chukchi." *American Ethnologist*, 36: 693–704.

Williams, J. (1999). *Unbending Gender: Why Family and Work Conflict and What to Do about It*. New York: Oxford University Press.

Williams, K. N., Kemper, S., & Hemmert, M. L. (2003). "Improving nursing home communication: An intervention to reduce elderspeak." *The Gerontologist*, 43: 242–247.

Williams, K. N., Herman, R., Gajewski, B., & Wilson, K. (2009). "Elderspeak communication: Impact on dementia care." *American Journal of Alzheimer's Disease and Other Dementias*, 24(1): 11–20.

Williams, K. N., Perkhounkova, Y., Herman, R., & Bossen, A. (2017). "A communication intervention to reduce resistiveness in dementia care: A cluster randomized controlled trial." *The Gerontologist*, 57(94): 707–718.

Williams, K. N., Shaw, C., Lee, A., Kim, S., Dinneen, E., Turk, M., Jao, Y., & Liu, W. (2017). "Voicing ageism in nursing home dementia care." *Journal of Gerontological Nursing*, 43(9): 16–20.

Williamson, J. B., & Rhodes, A. (2011). "A critical assessment of generational accounting and its contribution to the generational equity debate." *International Journal of Ageing and Later Life*, 6(1): 33–57.

Williamson, J. B., & Watts-Roy, D. M. (2009). "Aging Boomers, generational equity, and framing the debate over social security." In R. B. Hudson (Ed.), *Boomer Bust? Economic and Political Issues of the Graying Society*, pp. 153–169. Westport, CT: Praeger.

Williamson J. B., McNamara T. K., & Howling S. A. (2003). "Generational equity, generational interdependence, and the framing of the debate over social security reform." *Journal of Sociology and Social Welfare*, 30: 9–112.

Wilson, C. (2015). "Hollywood's glaring gender gap." Retrieved from http://time.com/4062700/hollywood-gender-gap/

Wolff, J. L., & Roter, D. L. (2011). "Family presence in routine medical visits: A meta-analytical review." *Social Science and Medicine*, 72: 823–831.

Wolff, J. L., Boyd, C. M., Gitlin, L. N., Bruce, M. L., & Roter, D. L. (2011). "Going it together: Persistence of older adults' accompaniment to physician visits by a family companion." *Journal of the American Geriatric Society*, 60: 106–112.

Woods, L. L. (2012). "The federal home loan bank board, redlining, and the national proliferation of racial lending discrimination, 1921–1960." *Journal of Urban History*, 38: 1036–1059.

Wu, C., Liu, Y., Chen, W. Y., & Wang, C. (2012). "Consumer responses to price discrimination: Discrimination bases, inequality status, and information disclosure timing influences." *Journal of Business Research*, 65: 106–116.

Yun, R. J., & Lachman, M. E. (2006). "Perceptions of aging in two cultures: Korean and American views on old age." *Journal of Cross-Cultural Gerontology*, 21: 55–70.

Zeckhauser, R., & Shepard, D. (1976). "Where now for saving lives?" *Law and Contemporary Problems*, 40(4): 5–45.

Zurcher, J. D., & Robinson, T. (2018). "From "Bibbid-bobbidi-boo" to Scrooge: An update and comparative analysis of the portrayal of older characters in recent Disney animated films." *Journal of Children and Media*, 12(1): 1–15.

Index

Age Discrimination in Employment Act 45, 107, 117, 119–122
ageism: ageism segments 68, 72, 74, 77–78, 128; fair innings ageism 90–91; institutional ageism 6–9, 129–130; peripheral ageism 65–66; succession ageism 119, 126; utilitarian ageism 90–91
age-restricted housing communities 8–9, 12, 66, 113–114, 124–126
authoritarian personality 17, 114

career development theory 105
communication accommodation theory 86
convergence theory 31
cultivation theory 68, 70–71
cumulative inequality 53, 55, 62, 107

discrimination: age discrimination 9, 122, 128–130; reverse discrimination 2–4; statistical discrimination 16, 27–28, 97, 100, 102–103; unintentional discrimination 2, 4–6
disparate impact 3
double jeopardy 56–59, 61

ecological model: chronosystem 81–82, 91–93; exosystem 81–82, 88–89, 92; macrosystem 81–82, 89–93; mesosystem 81–82, 88–89; microsystem 81–82, 84–88, 91–83; proximal processes 81–82, 92–93
elder abuse 117–119
elderspeak 4, 6, 9, 12, 81, 85–88, 92–93

filial responsibility law 13, 30, 37–38
frame: collective frame break 45–46; frame analysis 40–53, 66, 97, 104–106, 108, 111–112; generational equity frame 46–48, 50–51, 115–116, 129; generational interdependence frame 48–49, 51–52; ideal career frame 97, 104–106, 108, 128; ideal worker frame 97, 104–106, 108, 128; individual frame break 43–44; primary frames 42–44; secondary frames 42–45, 49

generational accounting 47–48

ideology, 66, 106–126
industrialization 31–33, 35–36
in-group 19–22, 101
intersectionality 14, 54–64, 66, 75, 97, 106–108, 112, 129

Matthew Effect 62–63
medicalization 65, 81, 82, 91–94; acute medicalization 92
modernization: authority shift 32, 35–36, 66, 96–97, 103–104, 108–112; modernization theory 31–32, 36; value modernization framework 30–39; well-being shift 32–33, 35–38, 103

out-group 19–22, 25, 97, 100–101

pension plans: employer pension plans, 10, 51; public pension plans, 122–124
political economy: aging enterprise 115–117; citizen/public 115–117; financial and post–industrial capital 115–118, 120; medical-industrial complex 115–118; sex/gender system 115–117, 121; state 114–126

preference reversals 42–43
productive aging 129–130

quality-adjusted life years 89–91

redlining 7–8
relational demography 21, 101–103

senior citizen discounts 2–4, 9
social identity theory *16*, 21–22, 83, 101
stereotype: self-stereotyping 82–83; stereotype buffering 58–59, 61, 63; stereotype content model *16*, 25–26, 56; stereotype segmentation 68; stereotype threat 82–84; substereotypes 59
subgrouping 14, *55*, 59–61, 63–64

terror management theory 13, 15–*16*, 22–24, 56; mortality salience hypothesis 22–23
Title VII of the Civil Rights Act 3, 7, 107, 120–122

youth cultures 68, 72–74, 78